FUNCTION, , AND SUBVERSION IN TYPOGRAPHY

FUNCTION, RESTRAINT, AND SUBVERSION IN TYPOGRAPHY

J. Namdev Hardisty
Princeton Architectural Press, New York

TABLE OF CONTENTS

In and Out *book, 2007 (Author: Jonathan
Ellery; Client: Browns Editions)
Designed by Browns*

Glass *CD, 2009 (Artist: Sissy Spacek;
Client: Misanthropic Agenda)
Designed by John Wiese*

Bassline *poster, 1997 (Client: Paradiso)
Designed by Experimental Jetset*

206 Studio Temp

220 Walker Art Center

232 John Wiese

238 YES

246 *Modern Poetry, Relative Poverty and Shimmers Of Hope* Experimental Jetset

250 *Acknowledgments*

252 *Biographies*

The Violence of Participation *book, 2007 (Editor: Markus Miessen; Client: Sternberg Press) Designed by Zak Kyes*

Songs of Love & Hate exhibition invitation, 2008 (Client: Ancient & Modern Gallery) Designed by A Practice For Everyday Life

Guy Tillim exhibition advertisement, 2008 (Client: Haunch of Venison) Designed by Spin

A DISCLAIMER IN FOUR PARTS
J. NAMDEV HARDISTY

The work in this book will resemble other books you have seen. They will have had titles containing keywords and phrases like *the new…*, *Minimalism*, *white space*, and *simplicity*. If this book was anything like those, it would unfold in the following fashion: I (or a noteworthy essayist) would claim that the work is a new trend/movement, that it is a reaction to X or a reemergence of Y, and that this book documents the future of graphic design. I would then use a certain thesis—aesthetic, theoretical, or otherwise—to prove my point. I would arrange and group the illustrations by aesthetic criteria that would give the impression of a mass movement creating similar work and exploring the same ideas. When all was done, I may even have convinced you that this is what your work should look like if you wanted to stay at the forefront of the field.

But this is not that book.

1. This book is not about a movement.

It doesn't aim to define one or create one. It is about a hundred micromovements with members that might occupy four of them at once or stick to their own agenda but claim no single flag. It is about Akzidenz Grotesk used in a specific manner, about subtle references to vernacular sources (like the "undesigned" flyers we see everyday on bulletin boards and telephone poles), about foregoing expressive compositions for expressive materials (surfaces like cardboard and foil or the use of die-cuts and new formats), about new typefaces used in old ways and old typefaces used in new ways, about type as image and image as type, about rendering a message in as clear a manner as possible, or not.

The pieces published here roughly fall under the umbrella of three isms: Brutalism, Modernism, and Minimalism. The work of some of the designers can easily be labeled as of one movement, others all three. And in each instance, there is a different reason for the categorization—a poster might display traits of Modernism, like a particular use of Helvetica, as well as Brutalism, while another might be similar but the choice of typeface is not Modernist. These are definitions in flux that apply to work free of a single ideology or viewpoint. There are pages in this book where a piece of design that looks like its maker channeled the ghost of Josef Müller-Brockmann sits next to a profoundly contemporary poster—both designed by the same person.

2. This is not a manifesto.

There is no single ideology at play in the work featured here. There are strands of thinking and opinions and taste. As such, this book was written without a core thesis. It is a collection of observations and opinions—my observations and opinions.

In some ways, this book is a piece of old-school art criticism—taking the work at face value, comparing it to what I know about graphic design, typography, and the designers themselves, I then

A DISCLAIMER IN FOUR PARTS
J. NAMDEV HARDISTY

draw conclusions. That is it. I don't claim to speak for the designers featured here, only about them.

And when I speak about them, I'm careful to avoid labeling them. In fact, when compiling this book, I asked each designer to contribute a minimum of three projects that best represent the range of their practice. Rather than simplifying a designer's style to a single, homogenous visual language, each one is presented with a selection of work, often with contradictory elements.

The designers featured here were chosen on the basis of having a body of work wherein ideas related to the central themes of Brutalism, Modernism, and Minimalism emerged again and again. The work of the American designers who make up MGMT., for example, was selected for the recurrence of classic Modernist forms. Their designs for the books *Building: 3000 Years of Design, Engineering and Construction* (2007) and *Archive Fever: Uses of the Document in Contemporary Art* (2008) refer to sixties Swiss Typography with their low-contrast hierarchies, lowercase sans-serif typefaces, and simple grids. The British studio YES was included for their overall approach to design. Though they utilize many styles for their projects, there is a distinct Minimalist strain that runs through the work. The French designers of Hey Ho maintain a Brutalist use of typography—condensed black type populates the surfaces of their projects with a near absence of imagery.

Each of these firms have a different reasoning for the visual outcome of their works, but they are all indicative of the new contemporary typography. For these designers, typography is no longer one of many elements that make up graphic design but the single most important element of design.

3. The sampling here is neither scientific nor exhaustive.

It is the work that I've been thinking about over the last few years. As blogs began to publish more and more work that revealed the influence of sixties Modernism as well as designs based purely on typography, I wondered about the relationship between those designs and the history of graphic design: Are those works an inevitable part of the lineage of Modernism or a tired rehash? How does this type of design function in contemporary society? Is it a response to sensory overload or an independent evolution of thought more concerned with language than image? These are crucial questions that reveal an important development in contemporary design, but one that has not been examined critically or in detail. It's not all the work I want to show and certainly not all the work that should be shown.

This book may seem highly Eurocentric—perhaps strange coming from the combination of an American author and publisher. It may be that there is a tangible difference between the design cultures of the North American and European continents, and that these types of differences are prevalent throughout the world. My encounters with Brazilian and Argentinian design have led me to believe that South America has an advertising-driven design culture similar to the United States, which may explain the absence of South American designers. I'm not sure. What I do know is that I have never given a FRS (Function Restraint Subversion) tag to a South American or African designer's website on Delicious.com, the social bookmarking site I used to keep track of research. I think that means something. But that's an essay for another day and some other purpose.

4. This is not the state of graphic design today.

It is one of many states of graphic design today. When looking at the feeds of the many design blogs that exist, it would be easy to assume that this is what graphic design looks like now. But really, this is only what some graphic design looks like.

These ideas are spreading only because a network of blogs and magazines has given so much attention to them. But the beauty of graphic design today is that there are dozens of movements emerging and reemerging and a wealth of different views on what contemporary graphic design is. This is not the future of graphic design. It is graphic design now.

And now we come to what this book may be about. This is a collection of designers whose work is about more than applying a style of Minimalism, Brutalism, or Modernism to a project—it is an expression of beliefs about what graphic design should look like and how it should function. Each of these designers define these beliefs differently—that a text should be more than "readable" (a standard of nineties typographic experimentation), that it should reflect a cultural lineage (building off of what has already been accomplished in the field of design), that it should be pared down to bare essentials (to respect the primacy of a text). These are designers with agendas. These are not designers who would do "anything for money" (to misappropriate a quote by the late Tibor Kalman). No, to create the bodies of work featured here requires dedication to those beliefs.

I don't think it will come as a surprise that 90 percent of the work featured here was not created for the louder-faster-brighter world of advertising and mass media, but rather falls under the vague umbrella category of "culture"—designs for museums and art galleries, for independent publishers, for schools, or produced as art projects. If these works grab your attention, it is likely due to the severe contrast of something so simple within our increasingly complicated world. They also speak to us on a human scale—while reading a book, navigating a museum, or ordering lunch. They reveal and illuminate rather than mask and distort.

In the end, this book is simple. It is a collection of the work of a group of designers driven by typography and a vision of typography that we haven't seen in a long time—one that favors readability and isn't afraid to look to the past for inspiration or guidance. These designers believe that the best way to say something is often the most straightforward, and that it is not always necessary to embellish or interpret a text. This book is one person's discussion of that work. Enjoy.

A PRACTICE FOR EVERYDAY LIFE

The London-based studio A Practice For Everyday Life (APFEL), founded by Kirsty Carter and Emma Thomas, craft simple and elegant designs based on careful observation of the subject matter and conversations with clients and collaborators. The resulting pieces are often quite minimal with a sly referential quality. Their invitation for the exhibition Wrong (Klosterfelde Gallery, Berlin, 2006) takes the curator's statement and sets it in a clean, almost default-document style. →01 In red they overlay onto the text the "invisibles," the software symbols that show what is happening in the spaces between words—the ends of paragraphs, word spaces, and soft returns. By working with the invisible spaces of graphic design, APFEL echoed the installation of the exhibition itself, which was set in a hallway at the gallery with the artwork hung salon style or informally placed. →02 This inconspicuous kind of reference—a tendency to make a gesture clear without pushing too far into the territory of a visual punch line—is consistent throughout APFEL's work.

Their posters for Cine Club (Thomas Dane Gallery, London, 2005–7), a series of film screenings, allude to the typography of film credits and the signage of old movie theaters but strip away the details so that what is left is a Minimalist interpretation of the original source. →03 The Cine Club logo uses the lines of a theater marquee as a simple graphic motif and lettering that references neon signage with a sans-serif outline reversed out of black, giving it a sense of being illuminated. The rest of the typography follows the convention of the credits on a film poster—justified typesetting on a centered axis. The result is a composition that is familiar but not clichéd. The references APFEL used created something new that goes beyond the original source.

For the outdoor installation *Proclamations*, a collaboration with writer Alain de Botton at The Yard Gallery (The Architecture Foundation, London, 2006), the firm took his pronouncements

→01 *Wrong exhibition invitation, 2006 (Client: Klosterfelde Gallery)* above *front detail* opposite left *front* opposite top right *back detail*

A bicycle wheel mounted on a stool (much smaller than the original).*

→02 *Wrong, 2006 (Exhibition installation at Klosterfelde Gallery)*

A PRACTICE FOR EVERYDAY LIFE

on architecture and beauty and rendered them as propaganda, albeit a very British one. Each statement lives alone in a rule-lined box set in either Futura or 3D Gill Sans, looking like a less-stylized version of the iconic Keep Calm and Carry On poster from World War II. →04 These pieces feel as if they should be at a diminutive scale—for a business card or handbill, perhaps—but blown up to three or six feet wide, they are disconcerting. Their stripped-down graphic language grows bolder, and they look more like wheat-pasted posters that were installed without permission—a protest against the architectural establishment.

Throughout their work, APFEL maintain a tension between the classic and the contemporary, the reference and the pastiche. It is in this space that they use graphic design to both point to other ideas and to ask questions about the nature of the object being viewed.

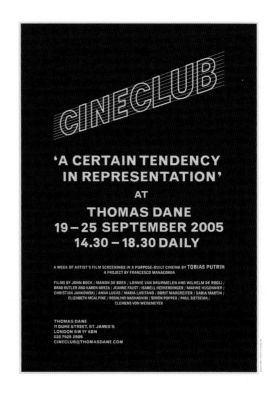

→03 *Cine Club exhibition invitation, 2005 (Client: Thomas Dane Gallery)*

→04 Proclamations *installation, 2006 (Collaboration with
Alain de Botton; Client: The Architecture Foundation)*

*The Scolt Head Screenings flyer, 2008 (Client:
Vanessa Desclaux and Isobel Harbison)*

A PRACTICE FOR EVERYDAY LIFE

Happy Hypocrite *magazine, 2008 (Client: Bookworks)*

The Happy Hypocrite

Linguistic Hardcore
Issue 1, Spring 2008

The Happy Hypocrite is published twice a year by Book Works.
Copyright Book Works, and the authors and artists © 2008.

No part of this publication may be reprinted or in any way reproduced without written permission from the publisher. The views expressed by the contributors are not necessarily those of the editor or the publisher.

ISBN 978-1-870699-93-1
ISSN 1755-475X

Editor
Maria Fusco

Art Direction & Design
APFEL (A Practice for Everyday Life)

Printing
Die Keure, Bruges

Sales & Distribution Manager
James Brook

Press & Marketing Manager
Gavin Everall

Intern
Charlotte Young

Advisory Board
Christopher Bretton, Jeff Dolven, Liam Gillick, Albert Mobilio, Sarah Pierce, Jane Rendell, Margaret Smith, Andrew Stephenson and Ardashir Vakil.

Welcome to the First Issue of The Happy Hypocrite

A THOUSAND AND ONE KNIGHTS OF THE ROUND TABLE OF KNOTTINGHAM

ALEXANDRE SINGH

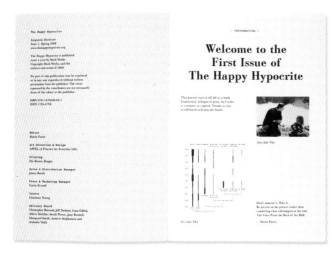

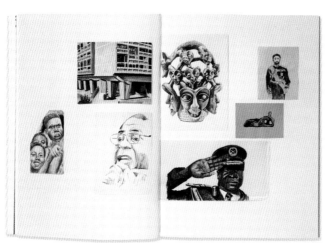

DOES TIME FEEL LONGER TO ANIMALS BECAUSE THEY DON'T HAVE WORDS TO ORGANISE THEIR EXPERIENCES?

A PRACTICE FOR EVERYDAY LIFE

The Architects' Journal *magazine, 2005 (Client: EMAP Communications)*

Costs

Data based on final account, for gross internal area

PREPARATION
Strip out and structural repairs £188.00/m²
General strip out and decommissioning. Extensive brickwork stitching and crack repairs. General strengthening work and steelwork repairs

SUBSTRUCTURE
Substructure and basement £187.40/m²
Tanking, damp-proofing and reinforced concrete power-floated basement slab. Drainage alterations. Lining basement walls

SUPERSTRUCTURE
Roof, rooflights £96.10/m²
New rear extension roof slab with exposed concrete soffit. Rooflights to rear studio. Single-ply membrane to studio and main roof
Staircases £26.90/m²
Refurbish existing timber stairs. New access stair to studio roof
External walls, windows, doors £238.40/m²
FET timber anodised aluminium/timber composite double glazing to elevations. New single-storey shop front with integral front door. Sto render to front and part rear. New brickwork and part repointing
Internal walls, partitions, doors £102.90/m²
Timber stud partitions, solid core flush doors. Insulated Gyproc lining to existing walls

INTERNAL FINISHES
Wall finishes £36.80/m²
Skim coat plaster and making-good existing
Floor finishes £74.40/m²
Levelling existing floors. Tongue-and-grooved plywood boarding. Linoleum
Ceiling finishes £41.30/m²
Glasroc ceiling linings and skim coat plaster

FITTINGS AND FURNISHINGS
Furniture £4.00/m²
Bathroom furniture, cabinets etc

SERVICES
Space heating, water supply, disposal, sanitary appliances, service equipment £127.70/m²
LPHW heating. New water supply and disposal. New utilities supplies
Electrical, protective services, lighting, communications installations £70.20/m²
Lighting and power throughout. Front door video entry system

PRELIMINARIES AND INSURANCES
Preliminaries £76.40/m²

Cost summary

Cost data provided by Brendan Hennessy Associates

	Cost per m2 (£)	Percentage of total
Preparation	188.00	15.79
Substructure	107.40	9.02
Roof, rooflights	96.10	8.07
Staircases	26.90	2.26
External walls, windows, doors	238.40	20.02
Internal walls, partitions	74.80	6.28
Internal doors	28.10	2.36
GROUP ELEMENT TOTAL	464.30	38.99
Wall finishes	36.80	3.09
Floor finishes	74.40	6.25
Ceiling finishes	41.30	3.47
GROUP ELEMENT TOTAL	152.50	12.81
Fittings and furnishings	4.00	0.35
Space heating, water supply, disposal, sanitary appliances, service equipment	127.70	10.72
Electrical, protective services, lighting, communications installation	70.20	5.90
GROUP ELEMENT TOTAL	197.90	16.62
Preliminaries and insurances	76.40	6.42
TOTAL	1,190.50	100.00

15. View of the split-level roof terrace: a secluded urban retreat

Credits

Tender date
June 2003
Start on site
July 2003 (contract duration 26 weeks)
Gross internal floor area
242m²
Form of Contract
Single-stage contract with JCT intermediate form
Total cost
£290,000
Architect
Tony Fretton Architects: Tony Fretton, Jim McKinney, Matt Barton, Karin Hepp, Simon Jones, David Owen
Structural engineer
Price & Myers
Cost consultant/quantity surveyor
Brendan Hennessy Associates
Main contractor
Famella
Subcontractors and suppliers
Render Sto Render; *render paint* Keim Mineral Paint; *glazing, skylights* Standard Patent Glazing Company, Luxcrete; *windows* FET; *access panels* Howe Green, ACO; *ironwork* Hargreaves, Thomas Dudley; *floor finishes* WISA Board, Forbo (linoleum); *ironmongery* Ize; *joinery* Famella; *ventilation* Ventaxia, Waterloo; *radiators* MHS, Hudevad; *sanitaryware* Ceramica Flaminia, Duravit, Kaldwei, Armitage Shanks; *taps* Vola, Pegler, Armitage Shanks; *electrical* MEM, Newey & Eyre; *entryphone* Entryphone London; *lighting* ER CO, Thorn, Concord, Newey & Eyre

---

CONTENTS

AJ SPECIFICATION

P. 25 TONY FRETTON

P. 50 FREI OTTO

P. 10 6A GALLERY

P. 14 CEDRIC PRICE

P. 66 BUDDY HAWARD

A SUBSCRIPTION TO THE AJ GIVES FREE ACCESS TO ALL OUR ONLINE SERVICES

BUILDING STUDY

AN OLD BOXER'S FACE, RAVISHED BY TIME AND EXPERIENCE, HOLDS ANOTHER KIND OF RAW, HONEST BEAUTY

by John Pawley. Photography by Daniel Gilbert

A PRACTICE FOR EVERYDAY LIFE

The Architects' Journal *magazine, 2006 & 2007 (Client: EMAP Communications)*

SONGS
OF
LOVE
& HATE

Songs of Love & Hate exhibition invitation, 2008 (Client: Ancient & Modern Gallery)

A PRACTICE FOR EVERYDAY LIFE

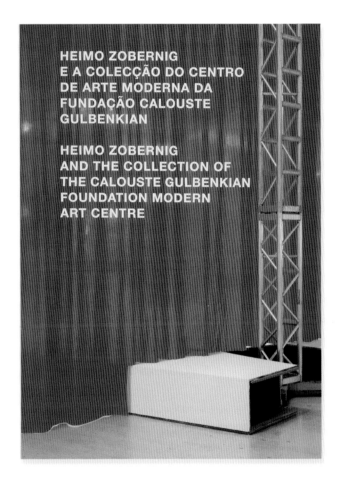
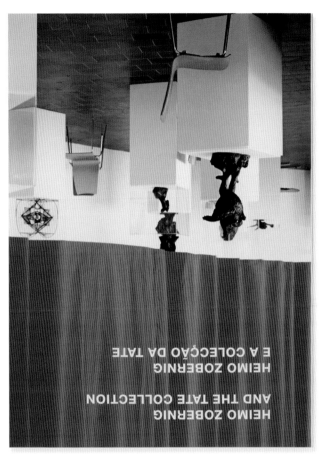

Heimo Zobernig and the Tate Collection/Heimo Zobernig and the Collection of the Calouste Gulbenkian Foundation Modern Art Centre *exhibition catalog, 2009 (Authors: Martin Clark, Jurgen Block; Client: Tate Publishing) The two catalogs are bound back to back as a single volume.*

HEIMO ZOBERNIG AND THE TATE COLLECTION / HEIMO ZOBERNIG E A COLECÇÃO DA TATE

But what is the image? When there is nothing, the image finds in this nothing its necessary condition, but there it disappears. The image needs the neutrality and the fading of the world; it wants everything to return to the indifferent deep where nothing is affirmed; it tends toward the intimacy of what still subsists in the void. This is its truth. But this truth exceeds it. What makes it possible is the limit where it ceases. Hence its critical aspect, the dramatic ambiguity it introduces and the brilliant lie for which it is reproached. It is surely a splendid power, Pascal says, which makes of eternity a nothing and of nothingness an eternity. – Maurice Blanchot

Since the late 1970s, Heimo Zobernig has developed a complex, interdependent practice that draws on various art historical movements and moments. He self-consciously revisits particular aesthetic discourses, often returning – perhaps perversely – to iconic and apparently irrepressible modernist motifs including Minimalism, the monochrome, colour theory, Constructivism and geometric abstraction. At the same time, he engages with ideas of architecture, design and display; in particular, with the way in which works of art are framed, both physically and conceptually, and how questions of form and function, use and uselessness, the 'real' and the replica, attend the object and the idea of the work in the world.

Zobernig's practice exploits the appearance of simplicity, employing a reduced, even sparse, aesthetic vocabulary. The 'prop-like' quality of his work is often cited with reference to his interest in theatre and set design, and many of his works seem to operate as surrogates or 'models', replicating or alluding to certain objects, images and ideas whilst simultaneously disrupting or undermining them. This is usually achieved through his use of mundane, domestic materials in the case of his sculpture; an apparently detached, programmatic and serial approach in his painting; or a subtle shift in function or intention, applied at various stages of his work's production and reception.

But they are 'prop-like' in another sense as well. Whether painting, sculpture, video, installation or design, Zobernig's works are invariably performative. They operate in and on the world as active, restless, and undecidable objects. They seem to exist in order to destabilise, agitate, provoke or propose – catalysts for, and the subject of, a rigorous but playful enquiry. In this way they call into question not just our subjective perception, but also a familiar litany of received ideological, practical, theoretical, social and art historical positions and conventions.

Zobernig's engagement with art and Modernism's various histories, alongside his interest in ideas of display, gave us the opportunity to think about the way in which we show the Tate Collection here in St Ives; about how, and what, we present in this very particular, and itself quite theatrical, building. It also allowed us to address the relationship of the St Ives School to a wider history of art and ideas stretching both backwards and forwards in time. Zobernig was invited to make his own selection from the Collection, and to consider how that selection might be 'framed' and displayed alongside his own works.

St Ives has a long and complex relationship with Modernism and its various revenants, residues and refugees. By the mid-twentieth century it had attracted a number of significant artists from all

over the world, becoming, for a time, an important centre both nationally and internationally. Its history, though, is shaped on the one hand by several important and influential personal relationships, while on the other, by the irresistible machinations of global events, including the outbreak of the Second World War. As a result, the influence of the European avant-garde and American Abstract Expressionism was filtered through the very particular experience of this remote Cornish fishing town, producing a series of extraordinary displacements and renegotiations; an ongoing cycle of eternal returns.

In his selection, Zobernig has included works by key figures associated with the colony in that fertile post-war period, including Barbara Hepworth, Naum Gabo, Patrick Heron, Terry Frost and Margaret Mellis. In addition he has chosen works by lesser-known artists like John Tunnard, Bob Law, Laura Knight, Anthony Hill and Ralph Rumney (a co-founder of the Situationist International) each of whom also had some greater or lesser association with the place. However these local connections were, more often than not, unbeknownst to Zobernig and of incidental curatorial interest. Much more important was a deeply personal response to the individual works themselves in an 'ahistorical', purely subjective and very specific way. From the outset, he approached the Collection in its broadest sense, drawing together a diverse and expansive group of works from the eighteenth, nineteenth and twentieth centuries.

In conversations, Zobernig spoke of an attraction to works which seem to represent or evoke some theatrical or dramatic sensibility, either through their composition, their subject, or even an 'atmosphere' (on one occasion he spoke about a talk he had attended by the architect and writer Mark Wigley that examined the atmospheric or meteorological conditions applied as a background to add 'mood' or 'drama' to architectural illustrations). Alongside this there was an interest in the unstructured aesthetic of Art Informel set against the rigour of geometric abstraction, a kind of form and formlessness running throughout his selection and across the centuries. He was also drawn to works that conceal a slightly uncertain status: remakes, stand-in's or propositions such as Marcel Duchamp's *Fountain*, an authorised replica refabricated in the 1960s after the lost original of 1917; Antoine Pevsner's *Maquette for a Monument Symbolising the Liberation of the Spirit* 1952; and perhaps most fascinating, an aluminium prototype Hepworth made as a trial for a later bronze, *Forms in Movement (Pavan)* 1956–9 (cast 1967). This object has remained on a work bench in the artist's St Ives studio since her death in 1975, and is shown here for the very first time.

It is easy to discern relationships to Zobernig's own practice here, evidenced through his overall approach to the selection, but there are resonances with individual works as well. Not just the geometric abstractions, monochromes and grids represented in pieces like Anthony Hill's *Orthogonal/Diagonal Composition* 1954, Bob Law's *No 62 (Black/Blue/Violet/Blue)* 1967 and Carl Andre's *144 Magnesium Square* 1969; but also in references to the body and fetish exemplified in works like Duchamp's *Female Fig Leaf* 1950 (cast 1961), Piero Manzoni's *Artist's Shit* 1961 or Karl Weschke's *Body on the Beach* 1977–8.[1] There are allusions to display and theatre in George Bernard O'Neill's *The Foundling* 1852, John Tunnard's *Reclamation* 1944 and Susanna Duncombe's *The Ghost Scene from 'The Castle of Otranto'* 1757; as well as an engagement with interior space, architecture and furniture evident, most strikingly, in Henry Wallis' *The Room in which Shakespeare was Born* 1853 – a work that, early on, became very important for Zobernig. He writes about it in a short text for *Tate Etc* magazine:

Looking for the void – for what's not there. Nothing found. I drew a blank... there is nothing in the centre of the room. And the centre of the painting is not only optically empty, creating a real spatial void, it's also empty as far as time is concerned. Is the empty space in the middle intended

BLANKA

Graphic designer Mark Blamire (see pages 138–45) started the online gallery and retail shop Blanka, which exhibits, publishes, and sells works that celebrate the legacy of twentieth-century Modernism. Blanka maintains an on-going repository of works by such influential Modernists as Otl Aicher, Wim Crouwel, and Josef Müller-Brockmann and showcases works by a new generation of designers—including Build, Spin, and Experimental Jetset—who continue the evolution of Modernist design. Blanka's exhibitions One: An Exhibition in Mono (2006) and 50 (2007)—the latter an exhibition celebrating the fiftieth anniversary of Helvetica—have toured throughout Europe and the United States. As a renewed interest in European Modernism has spread across the globe, Blanka has been ahead of the curve, shedding light on the roots of this movement and spreading the work of its best contemporary practitioners.

How did Blanka come about and when did it launch?
Blanka launched in December 2005. It came about
because of personal circumstances really. A year after
the birth of our son [Jack], my wife, Sharon, went back
to work full time. We had decided that I would work a
three-day week so that Jack would only be in childcare
part time. At that stage of my life, I had been a
graphic designer for fifteen years, and while I still
loved producing the work, I no longer enjoyed the slog
of chasing the clients. I realized that commission-
based graphic design wasn't achievable by working a
three-day week—you can't tell a client you are going
to miss a deadline or be unable to attend a meeting
because you are looking after children.

Simple was a really small label, but it had been a
fun experience. I had been involved with it alongside
doing my own design work at Neue, and it fit in nicely
when work was slow or I needed a distraction. It had
a very clear, straightforward business model: the
musicians delivered whatever songs they wanted to
put out and, instead of receiving an advance, they
got a 50 percent share in all of the profits from their
record sales. It was a great idea and meant that
everyone was treated equally and made the same
money. I also had a massive passion for posters and
poster design, and I had accumulated a healthy
collection over the years. Plus I had become good
friends with lots of other designers, who shared this
passion. So I decided to take the Simple model and
apply it to Blanka: the artists create beautiful prints
or sell work from their archives, and they get an equal
share of the profits. It's a simple philosophy, and it has
worked incredibly well with Blanka. It established a
little creative cooperative with lots of great individuals
combining their efforts and talents under one roof.

Was one of your aims to shed light on or spread your passion for Modernist design? Not at all, no. Modernism is a particular favorite subject of mine, but I also grew up reading comics and in my early years I was massively influenced by a broad spectrum of painters and illustrators. At college, I was inspired by the print and design work of Vaughan Oliver, who definitely can't be classified as a Modernist. Today there is a broad selection of styles and influences that still has an impact on me and that I am happy to promote. I love Modernism, but Blanka doesn't have a Modernist agenda at all. It's too narrow a subject to base your entire output of work around. Our goal is to spread the word of good craft and beautiful print. That's all, really.

Blanka acts as a publisher, distributor, and online gallery all at once. Do you have distinct aims or motivations with these different arms, or a single purpose? It's a single purpose. I don't see any distinction between making a T-shirt or a poster. If it's pleasing to my eye and I like it, we make it. Sometimes it's a T-shirt, sometimes it's a poster, or it could be a roll of masking tape. Hopefully, it's just about executing good ideas, and whatever format fits theidea best is what comes off of the production line. It's about bringing good ideas to life and hopefully inspiring people. That's our single purpose.

Through curating exhibitions and publishing, you work with many of the same designers and artists again and again. Obviously you admire their work, but do you also feel like you champion it? I suppose it could be viewed that way, but not really, no. I have chosen these artists because they are already champions of their own work, and they work with us because they believe in the Blanka ethos. We work with artists who have created their own destiny and are completely in control of their talent. We are just tapping into the work because we believe in the individuals, and we want to work with great people who are already at the top of their game.

Are you working against any tendencies in contemporary graphic design through Blanka? Not really. I have my own goals and tastes, which I prefer to move toward, but I am not reacting against anything or anybody. Work that I don't like simply doesn't make it onto the site. I work on the premise that if I wouldn't want to own a copy of something, then it doesn't make it onto Blanka.

There has been a resurgence of interest in Modernism over the last decade, especially in the last five years. Why do you think that is? Modernism is timeless. It's stylish, yet it doesn't rely on trends, hence its longevity. It created its own solid series of design principles and code of working. It emerged during the period of time directly after World War II. As a result, the people who founded the style established their own philosophy and belief system based on trying to rectify mistakes made by those that had come before. The movement had a real direction, affording it additional power and meaning. It's these qualities and principles that give it its timeless strength. The movement is far reaching and is embraced by graphic design, product design, architecture, and fashion. Its simplified approach and code make it easy to take up and follow. For those of us who need less visual clutter in our lives, Modernism is the perfect solution.

Has Blanka helped fuel this resurgence or is it simply a matter of good timing? Good timing.

Do you feel like you've seen a change in graphic design during the time Blanka's been open (2005–10)? I am not sure if I am best qualified to answer that question. I retired from graphic design, in the traditional sense as a commission-based business with paying clients, five years ago to pursue a slightly different direction, so my experience of any changes are somewhat limited. In forming Blanka I created my own unique bubble. I distanced myself from deadlines and the need for a paying client, which makes it difficult for me to know what has gone on in the industry. There have been massive changes going on in the last five years, and I guess designers have had to diversify and be more creative to survive. You could say that Blanka was my own way of diversifying, and it ended up becoming its own entity.

We make work the way we want to make it and when we feel like it. In graphic design it's down to when the client instructs you to do it, and the job can be cancelled at the eleventh hour due to budget cuts or other external forces. We don't encounter any of these problems. Even in the downturn, we have continued to make posters because we have wanted to make them, and customers have continued to buy them. The biggest problem we have faced in the last five years was having to change the paper stock of a poster due to a paper-mill closing. There has obviously been massive impact on the industry, but fortunately we haven't really been affected by it.

Where would you like to see Blanka in five years? Are there areas you'd like to go into that you haven't yet? Just to continue making great work and having fun. The work has been immensely rewarding and satisfying, and I feel like we have come a very long way in the first four years. We have had the 50 exhibition celebrating fifty years of Helvetica at the Design Museum (London, 2007), which felt like a real feather in our cap. We have had work from the exhibition on the front cover of the design-and-communications magazine *Creative Review*, which has had regular features on our work on an almost monthly basis. We've also traveled the globe putting on exhibitions and making new friends and meeting inspiring people—so if it stays exactly the same in five years time, I would be more than happy. I feel incredibly lucky doing what I do. We work with our heroes, and it's our intention to make great and inspiring work for others to enjoy. We have great fun doing it and are constantly learning. We try to push printing processes as far as we can. We get the occasional email congratulating us on the work we are doing, and this keeps us driving forward. If we can keep inspiring people and making them smile, then I am happy with that. What more could you ask for, really?

BROWNS

Browns—founded by designer Jonathan Ellery in 1998—combines a contemporary approach with a vintage aesthetic in its practice. The studio's reputation was first established through the design and publishing (through Browns Editions) of art books by illustrator Paul Davis and Ellery. The success of these book designs put them at the forefront of the design entrepreneurship (the notion that contemporary design practice could encompass both the traditional sale of services and a new entrepreneurial spirit was first heavily hinted at in publications like *Eye* and *Emigre* in the 1990s).

Designers creating their own products and publications has now become a widespread phenomena. Browns carries out this very contemporary agenda while crafting visuals that blend Classical typography with Modernism. There is a consistency in bold treatments of traditional typefaces in the work that feels as though it points to other periods. The covers of the *Browns Paper* (1999–2005)—self-published broadsheets that promote the studio's recent projects—call to mind the American Modernist typography of *Architectural Review*, while the simple Brutalism of Ellery's *In and Out* (2007) and *136 Points of Reference* (2005) clearly relates to the International Typographic Style of the 1960s, with one typeface of a single weight and size placed in the most logical area—the upper left-hand corner. →01 & 02

That Browns avoids the pursuit of formal invention and shuns the strict reproduction of retro styles lends to the staying power of the work. There is a balancing act in it—an allegiance to the past but not a devotion to it.

Another factor at play here is the purist intention visible in their work. Books like Paul Davis's *God Knows* (2008) do not exhibit the expressive design-for-design's-sake graphic expositions that are evoked when the words *self-publishing* and *graphic designer*

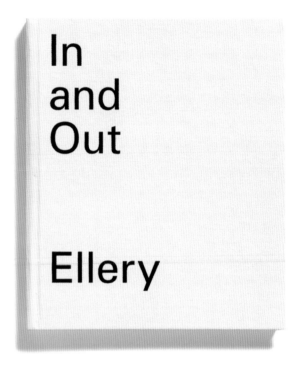

→01 In and Out *book, 2007 (Author: Jonathan Ellery; Client: Browns Editions; Design: Jonathan Ellery and Claire Warner)*

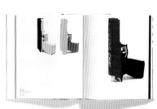

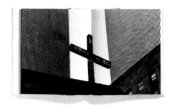

→02 136 Points of Reference *book, 2005 (Author: Jonathan Ellery; Client: Browns Editions; Design: Jonathan Ellery and Lisa Smith)*

are mentioned together. →03 They are books that are simply well designed and that treat their chosen subject matter with grace and care.

This grace and care is a cornerstone of Browns's approach. Not concerned with styles, Browns is instead concerned with the audience of these books, the readers consuming the images and living with them and the artists who took the photographs, drew the drawings, and wrote the words. In many ways, the core of the entrepreneurial projects of Browns is its concern with objects that are service-oriented: Browns always remembers the reader and makes sure that the design does not overshadow the ideas.

→03 above, and opposite top and center rows
God Knows *artist's catalog, 2005 (Author: Paul Davis; Client: Browns Editions; Art Direction: Nick Jones; Design: Nick Jones and Stephen McGilvray)*

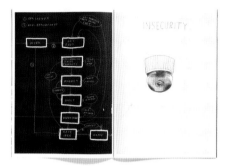

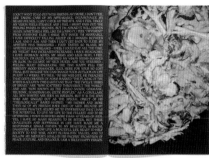

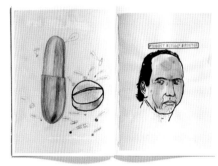

Nåtiønàl Intérprẽtinğ Sërviçê

above *National Interpreting Service logo, 2001 (Client: National Interpreting Service; Design: Scott Miller)*

BROWNS

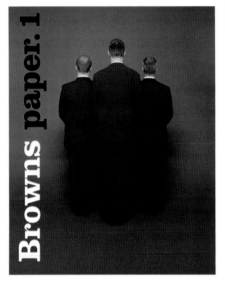

Browns Paper *magazine, 1999–2005 (Client: Browns)*

From Here To There *promotional book, 2003 (Author/Client: MacDonald Egan; Design: Jonathan Ellery and Scott Miller)*

BROWNS

John Jones identity system, 2009 (Client: John Jones;
Design: Jonathan Ellery and Claire Warner)

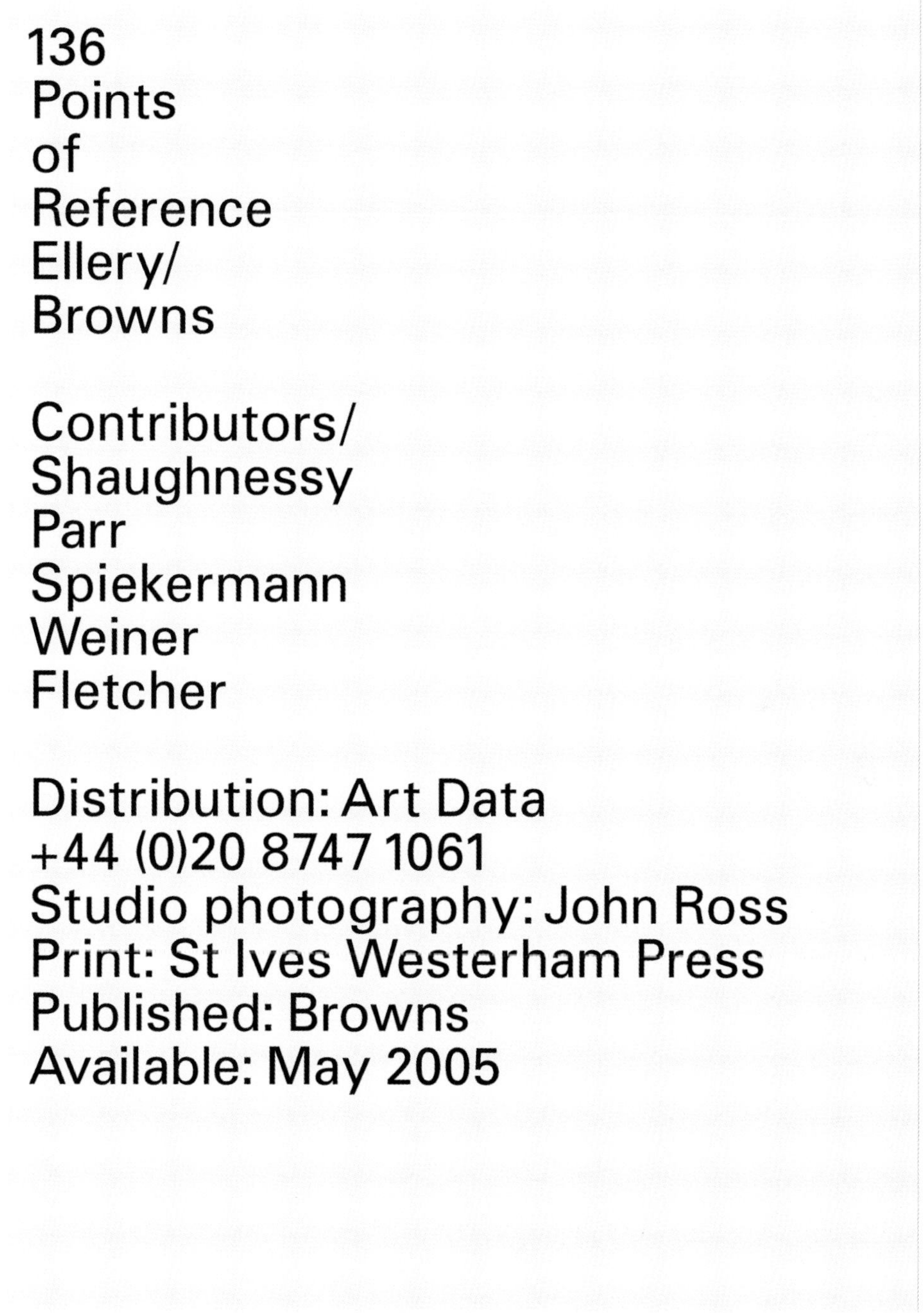

136
Points
of
Reference
Ellery/
Browns

Contributors/
Shaughnessy
Parr
Spiekermann
Weiner
Fletcher

Distribution: Art Data
+44 (0)20 8747 1061
Studio photography: John Ross
Print: St Ives Westerham Press
Published: Browns
Available: May 2005

136 Points of Reference poster, 2005 (Client: Browns Editions;
Design: Jonathan Ellery and Lisa Smith)

Eighty Seven

A new book by Jonathan Ellery
Available July 2006

Distributed internationally by Art Data
+44 (0)20 8747 1061
Printed by St Ives Westerham Press
www.westerhampress.co.uk

Published by Ellery/Browns

Eighty Seven poster, 2006 (Client: Browns Editions;
Design: Jonathan Ellery and Rachel Veniard)

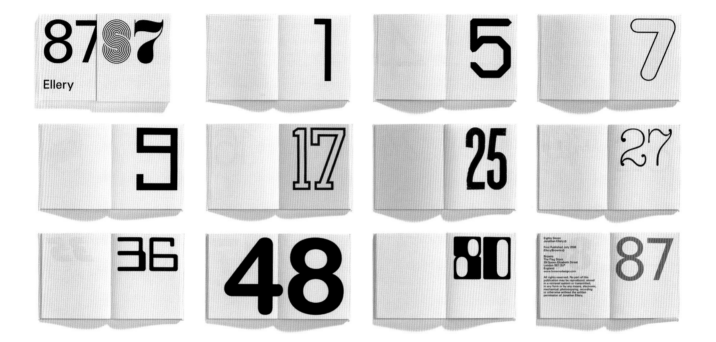

Eighty Seven book, 2006 (Author: Jonathan Ellery; Client: Browns Editions; Design: Jonathan Ellery and Rachel Veniard)

Browns: A Walk Through Books *book, 2002 (Author: Peter Kirby;*
Client: GCE Publishers; Design: Jonathan Ellery)

Browns
A walk through books

This is a book of type
Clumpy Ole Clarendon
Hob-nail-boot-font
So uncool it's untrue
Became the bully of Helvy
And now slaps its size fifteens
All over town

B

Published by GCE
Written by Peter Kirby
Printed by Westerham Press
Available February 2003
www.directions.ch

gce/directions **4**

Browns: A Walk Through Books poster, 2002 (Client: GCE Publishers; Design: Jonathan Ellery)

ANTHONY BURRILL

Anthony Burrill's most famous work may be his Popular Aphorisms, a series of posters illustrating simple truisms. →01 Woodblock letters were used to spell out Burrill's ideas about life and work on these text-only prints. Themes include Work Hard & Be Nice to People, Work Is Play, and It Is OK for Me to Have Everything I Want, among others. Four of these posters (eight total) eventually became limited-edition covers for *Wallpaper** magazine, an honor not usually bestowed on a purely typographic design. →02 But it isn't hard to see why they were chosen. Burrill chooses bold and dynamic typefaces and works the surface of the page—his typography, even at this level of simplicity, has the force of a great image.

Of course, the real story of Burrill's work is the iconic—whether illustrative, typographic, or language-based. In a series of advertisements for Hans Brinker Budget Hotel (produced with Dutch agency KesselsKramer), a silhouette of modern mass-produced product sits centered in a tasteful Modernist composition. →03 Each item is broken in some way—a missing tine on a fork, a straw that is bent, or a fiberglass shell chair with only three legs—and sits above the slogan "Unique Design." An earlier campaign bragged about features that would normally be taken for granted, such as working toilets. "Now Free Toilet Flushing" is accompanied by an illustration rendered in the anonymous style of the graphics found on cardboard boxes. →04 For his Put It Back exhibition at Concrete Hermit Gallery (London, 2007), Burrill distilled the vocabulary of all protests down to three signs: "Yes," "No," and a directional arrow. →05 With these three placards, you could easily protest or support just about any cause. But the oversized signs are installed as a collage on the wall, perhaps suggesting the futility of public protest.

Elsewhere in his work, Burrill is concerned with the tension between what a message looks like and what it says. The Bad Art series, for example,

→01 *From the Popular Aphorisms poster series, 2008 (Client: self-published)*

YOU KNOW MORE THAN YOU THINK YOU DO

Anthony Burrill for the RSA

ANTHONY BURRILL

perplexes viewers with graphically treated texts, a la Popular Aphorisms, juxtaposed to nonsensical type-image pictures. →06 Beyond the common color palette, it's not clear what makes the individual posters a collection of "bad art." It might simply be self-deprecation at play, or it might be a statement about expectations: the piece Bad Art—a sun setting over rolling hills beneath the words "Bad Art"—may be an illustration of bad art, the banal, mundane images that we universally accept as pretty. Then again, the banal and mundane is where Burrill gets his inspiration. He forces the viewer to think about the actual meaning of things that are taken for granted.

→02 Wallpaper* *magazine cover, 2008*
(Client: Wallpaper)*

→03 *Now Free Toilet Flushing poster, 1996 (Client: Hans Brinker Budget Hotel)*

ANTHONY BURRILL

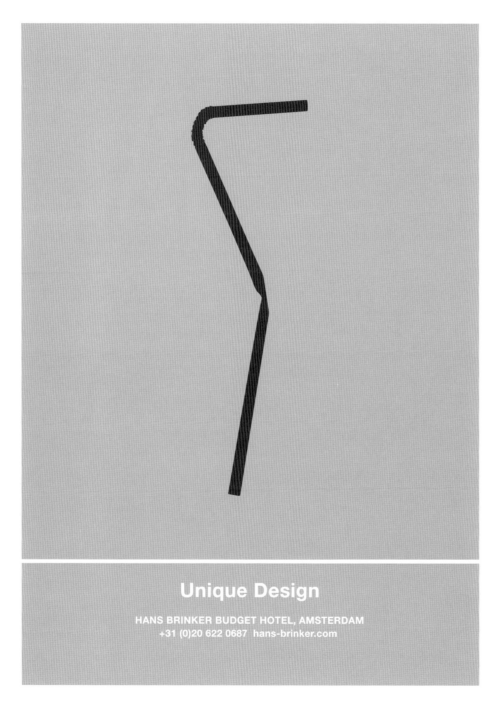

Unique Design

HANS BRINKER BUDGET HOTEL, AMSTERDAM
+31 (0)20 622 0687 hans-brinker.com

→04 *From the Unique Design poster series, 2006 (Client: Hans Brinker Budget Hotel)*

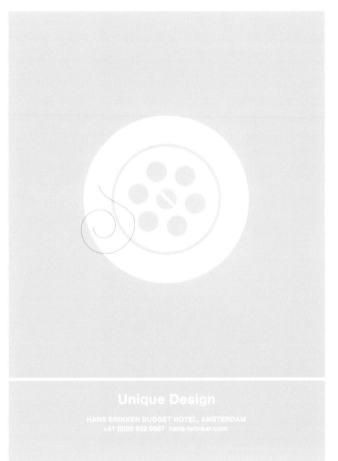

Unique Design

HANS BRINKER BUDGET HOTEL, AMSTERDAM
+31 (0)20 622 0687 hans-brinker.com

Unique Design

HANS BRINKER BUDGET HOTEL, AMSTERDAM
+31 (0)20 622 0687 hans-brinker.com

ANTHONY BURRILL

→05 *Put It Back exhibition, 2007 (Client: Concrete Hermit Gallery)*

→06 *From the Bad Art poster series, 2008 (Client: self-published)*

ANTHONY BURRILL

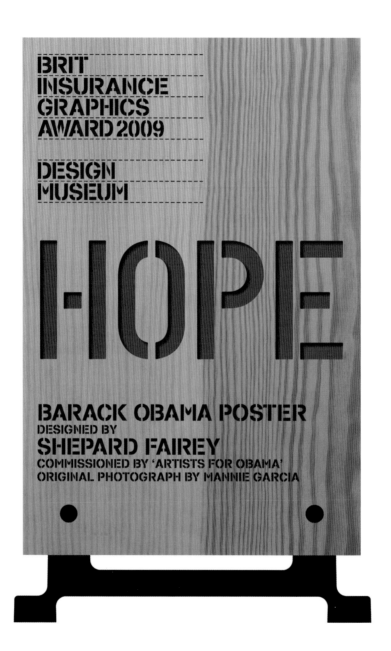

Design Museum award, 2009 (Collaboration with Michael Marriott;
Client: Design Museum)

FREE SPEECH
(TICKETS £10.00)

TAKING LIBERTIES
THE STRUGGLE FOR BRITAIN'S
FREEDOMS AND RIGHTS

31st October 2008 – 1st March 2009
King's Cross, St. Pancras and Euston
www.bl.uk/takingliberties

BRITISH LIBRARY

From the Taking Liberties poster series, 2009 (Client: British Library)

DANIEL EATOCK

Daniel Eatock regularly refers to Lucy Lippard's book on Conceptual and Minimalist art, *Six Years: The Dematerialization of the Art Object* (1973), as his favorite book. The cover of the book is solid red with white sans-serif type that fills the whole surface with the complete title of the work.[1] It is telling that Eatock's favorite book is not just a seminal text, but it is a book whose very cover embodies the ideas contained within it. The cover begins with an idea—communicating explicitly the book content in a profoundly direct manner. To say that there are parallels between *Six Years* and Eatock's work is an understatement.

Eatock's use of typography is little discussed because typography is not his focus. It is often incidental, a purely functional element to express a larger concept. The ideas that form Eatock's work have been hugely influential, especially among design students, since his now defunct Foundation33 website first showcased his Conceptual art–inspired approach to design. Eatock and his partner, Sam Solhaug, founded Foundation33 in 1999, and their website was known for showcasing a diverse range of activities without boundaries between disciplines. These activities ranged from their 10.2 Multi-Ply table (2000)—constructed from a single sheet of plywood cut into equal-sized slats, without waste—to the identity for the BBC television program *Big Brother* (2001) and the list *All the people who have inspired me, who I do not personally know, compiled from memory on 20 December 2001 São Paulo, Brazil* collected entirely through images found on the Internet. Since forming Eatock Ltd. in 2003, he has invited people to contribute to some of their ongoing projects on eatock.com.[2] There are scores of students whose websites document some everyday phenomena— making new mixtapes from random cassette tapes found on the street, documenting haircuts, or publishing collections of Mona Lisa reproductions— inspired by Eatock projects like Considered Accidents,

→01 *From the Considered Accidents photography series, 2000–2009 (Client: self-published)*

UTILITARIAN (DELETE AS NECESSARY) ADVERTISEMENT/ANNOUNCEMENT/BULLETIN/DECLARATION/PROCLAMATION

THIS POSTER PROVIDES A FRAME & STRUCTURE FOR THE INFORMATION & DETAILS FOR ANY EVENT/HAPPENING
COMPLETE THE EIGHT SECTIONS BELOW USING ANY METHOD OR MEDIUM
CONCEPT & DESIGN COPYRIGHT DANIEL EATOCK 1998 SAY YES TO FUN & FUNCTION & NO TO SEDUCTIVE IMAGERY & COLOUR!

TITLE

DESCRIPTION OF EVENT/HAPPENING

DATE

DIAGRAM/DOODLE/DRAWING/IMAGE/PAINTING/PHOTOGRAPH/SCRIBBLE/ETCETERA

LOCATION/ADDRESS

DIRECTIONS/MAP

FURTHER INFORMATION

IF YOU WOULD LIKE COPIES OF THE UTILITARIAN POSTER FOR ANY FORTHCOMING EVENT/HAPPENING CONTACT:
DANIEL EATOCK/SCHOOL OF COMMUNICATION DESIGN/ROYAL COLLEGE OF ART/KENSINGTON GORE/LONDON/SW7 2EU/UNITED KINGDOM
TELEPHONE + 44 171 590 4444 EXTENSION 4311/FACSIMILE + 44 171 590 4300

POSTER COMPLETED BY

→02 Utilitarian Poster *template, 1999 (Client: self-published)*

DANIEL EATOCK

a series of photographs documenting "complementary" dents on Fiat cars. →01

But his influence extends beyond conceptual ideas. The current interest in Swiss Typography is due in no small part to the formal qualities of Eatock's most iconic design work. In the late nineties he produced *Utilitarian Poster*, a generic template with preformatted spaces to allow anyone to create a poster for an event without designing one. →02 In addition to fulfilling some of the practical concerns of late Swiss Typography—the use of sans-serif type, a clear and organized grid, and a rational ordering of information—it is also a visual example of classic Swiss Typography, albeit with a sense of humor. There is nothing flashy about Eatock's design; it only does what it needs to. *Utilitarian Poster* even contains the philosophy that governs his work: "Say YES to fun & function & NO to seductive imagery & color."

In 2002 he created *The World's Largest Signed and Numbered Limited Edition Artwork*, a million-edition postcard. →03 This and *Utilitarian Greeting Cards* (2003) are even more firmly cemented in the framework of Swiss Typography, right down to the use of all lower-case Akzidenz Grotesk. →04 His use of this style was never about aesthetics but about making the design invisible or neutral. Many would argue (and rightly so) that any choice of typeface or color or composition affects the reading of a text. Eatock's use of a high-Modernist style, using white, black, and red sans-serif type, isn't inherently neutral or undesigned. But it is a collection of strategies that indicates the primacy of the text as his main goal. He takes late Swiss Typography and strips it down to its barest essentials that say, "read me."

But, over the last five years, there has been a growing trend of fetishizing Modernist typography. Documentaries like *Helvetica* (2007) and daily blog posts dedicated to posters about Akzidenz Grotesk undermine the reading of Eatock's undesigned works as pure concept and threaten to relegate them to the

→03 above and opposite top **The World's Largest Signed and Numbered Limited Edition Artwork** *postcard, 2002 (Client: self-published)*

The world's largest signed and numbered limited edition artwork

Authorised signatory

Daniel Eatock, Sam Solhaug, Hanna Werning, Lyn Winter, Flávia Müller Medeiros, Mark Hopkins, Soo Hong, Milos Covic, Naoko Sato, Kirsty Carter

Your number is

/One million

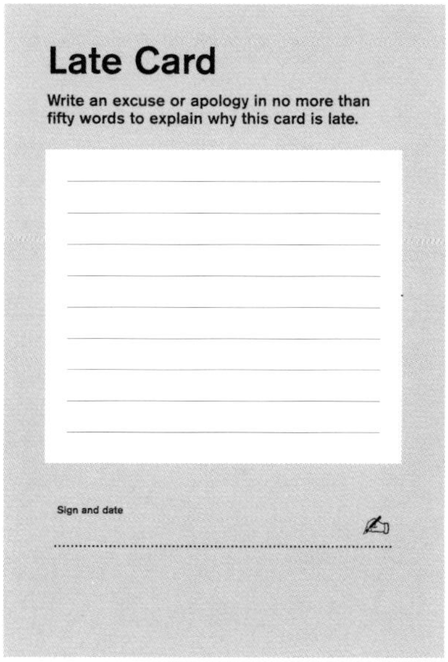

Late Card

Write an excuse or apology in no more than fifty words to explain why this card is late.

Sign and date

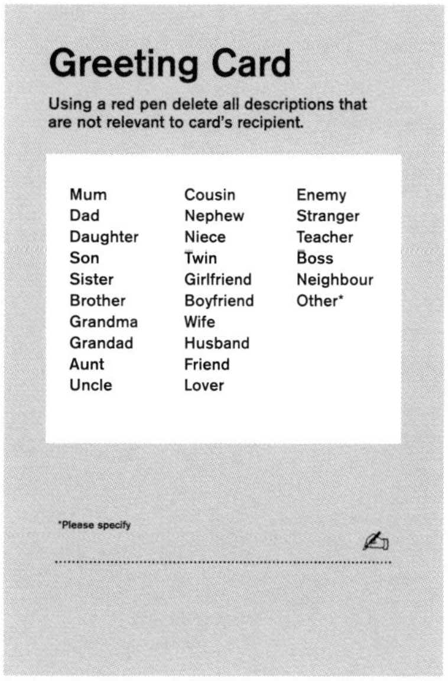

Greeting Card

Using a red pen delete all descriptions that are not relevant to card's recipient.

Mum	Cousin	Enemy
Dad	Nephew	Stranger
Daughter	Niece	Teacher
Son	Twin	Boss
Sister	Girlfriend	Neighbour
Brother	Boyfriend	Other*
Grandma	Wife	
Grandad	Husband	
Aunt	Friend	
Uncle	Lover	

*Please specify

→04 Utilitarian Greeting Cards, *2003 (Client: self-published)*

DANIEL EATOCK

category of just another cool thing to blog about. It's for this very reason that Eatock has steadily moved away from this aesthetic. A few years ago he produced a T-shirt that read "Fuck Graphic Design." Set in a default underlined, italicized Courier, it clearly articulates his opposition to design that is preoccupied with form. In recent graphic design works, like his monograph *Imprint* (2008), he uses a less-recognizable sans-serif type with virtually no variance in size and weight, downplaying the importance of a "beautiful" page design of contrast and typographic minutiae. →05

Throughout his career, Eatock has been dedicated to ideas that "allow concepts to determine form."[3] It seems that his further stripping away of superfluous elements, like the traditional approach to typography with its emphasis on visual tension through typographic contrast, is bringing his graphic design ever more in line with the unadorned sculptures, lists, and photographs that make up so much of his work.

NOTES

1. The cover actually reads "Six Years: The dematerialization of the art object from 1966 to 1972: a cross-reference book of information on some esthetic boundaries: consisting of a bibliography into which are inserted a fragmented text, art works, documents, interviews, and symposia, arranged chronologically and focused on so-called conceptual or information or idea art with mentions of such vaguely designated areas as minimal, anti-form, systems, earth, or process art, occurring now in the Americas, Europe, England, Australia, and Asia (with occasional political overtones), edited and annotated by Lucy R. Lippard."

2. Daniel Eatock's official website, http://www.danieleatock.com/project/daniel-eatock/.

3. Daniel Eatock, interview with the author, 2009.

→05 above, and opposite top and bottom left
Imprint *book, 2008 (Author: Daniel Eatock; Client: Princeton Architectural Press)*

I arranged a complete set of Letraset Tria Pantone markers in the order of the color spectrum and left them for one month, resting on their nibs, on a stack of five hundred SRA1 sheets of 70 gsm uncoated white paper.

The numbering and value of each sheet corresponds to its position within the stack. The final sheet the ink reached (out of the stack of five hundred) was numbered 1/73 and valued at one pound; the one above it was numbered 2/73 and valued at two pounds; and so on. The top sheet (the sheet the pens rested on directly) was numbered 73/73 and valued at seventy-three pounds.

Print 68 of 73

Untitled
Don Matheson and Simon Jones

Black and Gold Sign / Black and Gold Bin

Black Chair and Bin / Gold Foam and Graffiti
Picture of the Week

Design a pattern for a butterfly wing.
Deadline: tomorrow

Rubbish Flower
Picture of the Week

104   105

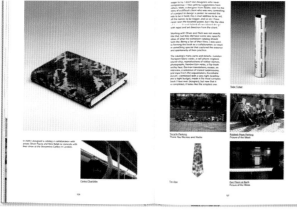

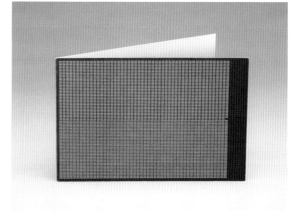

Millenium card, 1999 (Client: Walker Art Center)

DANIEL EATOCK

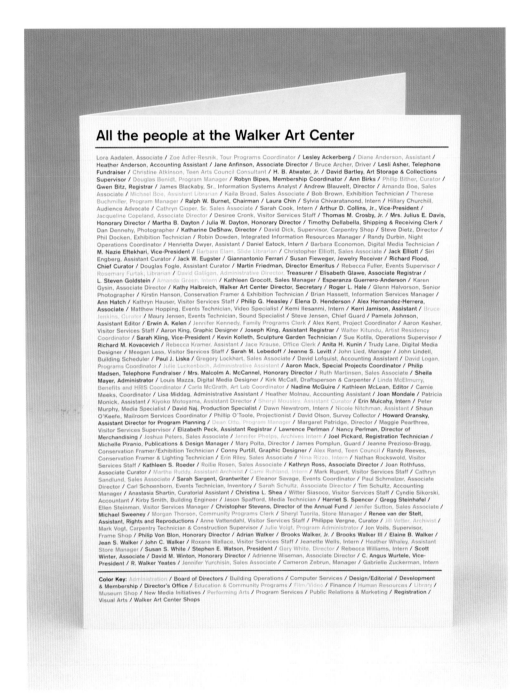

New Year 1999 card, 1998 (Client: Walker Art Center)

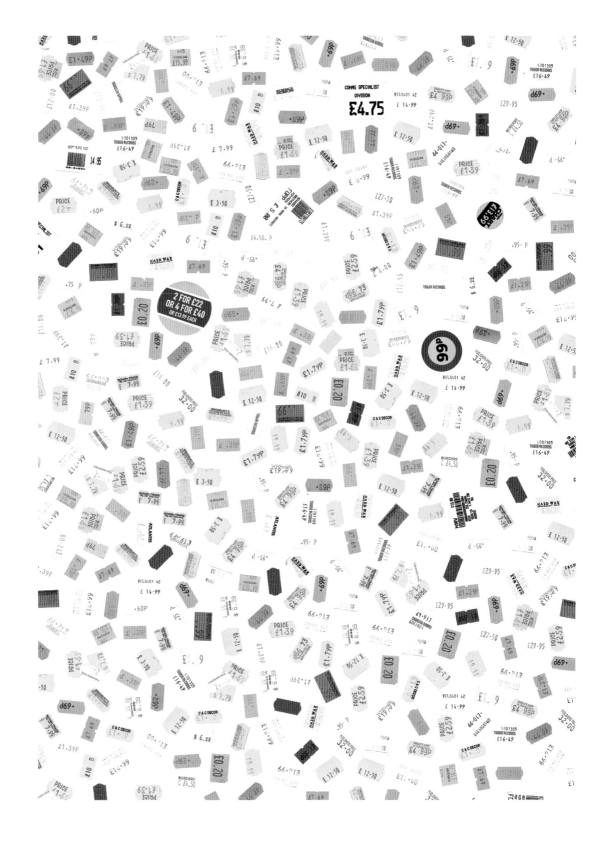

Price label gift wrap, 2003 (Client: self-published)

XAVIER ENCINAS

Xavier Encinas's Swiss Legacy blog, along with the design blogs September Industry and Aisle One, has kick-started a movement of a redefined Modernism that fuses the International Typographic Style with high-end materials—foils, blind embossing, and high-gloss surfaces. It comes as no surprise that Encinas's own design work shares these attributes. His printed works announce their physical presence—whether reflective or textured—before anything else and are imprinted with a crisp, stylized typography.

In his more Helvetica-anchored pieces like the poster Das Erbe der Schwiez (The heritage of Switzerland, 2009), the results are not very surprising—a competent marriage of Modernist typography with luxe materials like a flood of metallic ink and gloss varnishes—but it is in his work for the fashion quarterly *Under The Influence* (2009) that his abilities as a typographer really begin to shine. →01 & 02 Reflecting a more pluralist approach to layout and typography, *Under The Influence* takes the new weird typography most often celebrated by the blog Manystuff and filters it through Encinas's extremely detailed approach to graphic design, which results in an idiosyncratic design of typographic experimentation and spacious Modernist compositions. In issue 5, LTC Obelysk Grotesk is employed as the main typeface, a font most often selected to evoke the thirties. Page after page Encinas finds ways to use this typeface anew without resorting to customization or illustration. With a sparse palette he creates a magazine of remarkable visual depth.

For another editorial project, *The Lab Magazine* (2009), Encinas uses a mix of Classical and Modernist forms, a mix of centered headlines and introductions and left-justified text columns to create an intriguing typographic texture. →03 The photography is layered underneath or around the text, creating surprising compositions that give the magazine a very informal feeling.

→01 *Das Erbe der Schwiez poster (The heritage of Switzerland), 2009 (Client: self-published)*

→02 Under The Influence *magazine, 2009 (Client: Under The Influence)*

XAVIER ENCINAS

Encinas's designs have developed into an interesting fusion of Modernist typography and an eclectic taste for display typefaces. His projects maintain a clarity that comes from his grounding in Modernist principles of order, balance, and contrast, juxtaposed with references to a diverse range of influences.

→03 The Lab Magazine, *2009 (Client: The Lab Magazine)*

XAVIER ENCINAS

Soleil Noir identity system, 2009 (Client: Soleil Noir)

Grotesque poster, 2008 (Client: self-published)

EXPERIMENTAL JETSET

The Dutch design studio Experimental Jetset formed in 1998 when collaborators Marieke Stolk and Danny van den Dungen asked Erwin Brinkers to help them redesign the lifestyle magazine *Blvd*. Since then the group has developed a body of work and texts and interviews that have established them as one of the most influential design studios of the last decade. Projects like the *Kelly 1:1* art installation (Casco, Utrecht, 2002), the John&Paul&Ringo&George T-shirt (2001), the Stedelijk Museum CS (Amsterdam, 2004) identity system, and a slew of posters for various themed exhibitions have showcased the group's talent for creating profound graphic works from simple concepts that also propagate their bold, almost Pop Art, take on Modernism. →01 (Many people believe Experimental Jetset's work to be a wholesale appropriation of sixties International Typographic Style design, and I would argue that they couldn't be more wrong. There's a bold expressiveness to Experimental Jetset's work that is the result of high-contrast elements: black on white, bold versus light, big versus small. What makes their work the opposite of Minimalism is that the elements that are present are so high-impact that there's no need for anything else. Compare this to the sixties Swiss Typography that tended to be much more even-keeled.) While there is visual range in their work, they have, in general, developed an aesthetic that is recognizable as "the Experimental Jetset."

In 2008 they relaunched their website, which includes documentation of their earliest work—flyers and posters for the rock club Paradiso. Stolk and van den Dungen had begun collaborating on promotional material for Paradiso in 1996, and the studio continued to work for them through 1999. The Paradiso work, which has not been seen widely outside of the Netherlands, provides a glimpse into the development of the Experimental Jetset aesthetic, formally and conceptually.

→01 Kelly 1:1 *installation, 2002 (Client: Casco)*

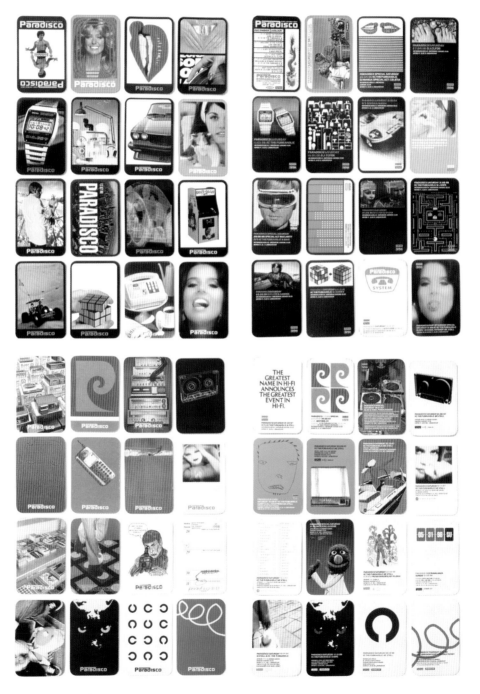

→02 *Paradisco flyers, 1996 (Client: Paradiso)*

EXPERIMENTAL JETSET

The earliest series of flyers for Paradisco, a monthly disco party, evoke little of the sensibility of the Experimental Jetset of today. →02 These pocket-sized flyers are image-heavy and use appropriated imagery from the seventies and eighties to support the disco theme—there's no bold Helvetica or Futura in sight. But traces of their thinking about pieces of graphic design as a three-dimensional object, where every plane has a relationship to the others, are present in this work. The flyers were conceived of as two-sided "frames" that hold images, and while there is an aura of kitsch (especially those designed in the first year), they also attempted to create "visual poetry." Each flyer has a core integrity even if the subject matter is silly—snow bunnies or Bruce Lee, for example. Eventually they moved away from the disco associations and began to explore the visual/verbal puns, Modernist forms, and exposed white space that has come to mark their work.

Over the course of a few years (roughly 1996 to 1998) more of the ideas and gestures that have become the hallmark of the firm's work were more clearly defined. The Paradisco's monthly calendar of events, started in 1996, explores the idea of graphic design as an object. →03 A check box, which is die cut into the paper, sits next to the name of each event; when these posters are hung, the layers of posters and flyers underneath show through. The hole in the sheet references the rich layers of artifacts living on the walls of Amsterdam. These posters also mark the introduction of Helvetica into their work. Although Experimental Jetset's work is perceived to be synonymous with Helvetica, it is actually Helvetica Neue 75 Bold (which first appears with the Bassline posters mentioned below) with which the group is associated—and a particularly Brutalist application of it. The use of the extended weight coupled with the all-lowercase typesetting and muted color palettes creates a feel of vintage Modernism. Furthermore, the type is used in a very traditional manner—a great

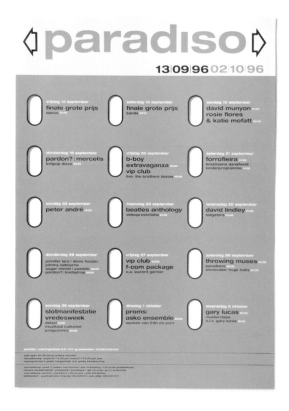

→03 *Paradiso program poster, 1996 (Client: Paradiso)*

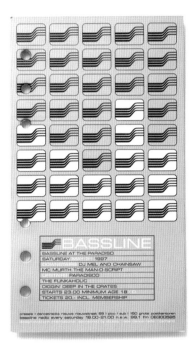

→04 *Bassline flyers, 1997 (Client: Paradiso)*

EXPERIMENTAL JETSET

deal of typographic detailing in terms of hierarchy, scale changes, and color usage—which adds a "fussiness" when compared to the visual brashness that their work has articulated in recent years.

The flyers for the hip-hop nightclub Bassline (1997) are where their aesthetic—the combination of form and language—really begins to emerge. →04 The Bassline flyers originally began as a riff on Filofax sheets, and a "cold" corporate identity was devised so that that the flyers would read as a mass-produced object. The backsides contain plays on the functions of the Filofax—ruled paper, lined paper, or other types of information holders. These pieces are the first instances of the group working with Modernist forms in a significant way. After all, both the stripped-down information design and the highly recognizable corporate identity were key developments of the International Typographic Style of the sixties and seventies. The front sides of the flyers are pitch-perfect replicas of seventies corporate identity with an abstract logo that is open to interpretation.

Around 1998 the Bassline flyers changed dramatically. →05 Through the introduction of Helvetica Neue Bold, color overlays, and found images that evoke the sixties, they became softer, brighter, and simpler. It's at this point that they began to find an alternative Modernist form to the colder corporate Modernism they were first experimenting with. While many regarded the reductive visuals and simplified typography of high Modernism as incapable of being anything besides cold and impersonal, Experimental Jetset, like designer Mike Mills at roughly the same time in the United States (see pages 120–27), found within it something friendly and bright, a so-called soft Modernism that was certainly more human than the Postmodern ideology of the time. This work is where we see the Experimental Jetset of today come into frame. Now, rather than using words to advertise the event explicitly, the headlines are free associations—"BassLine. Lemon and Lime." or

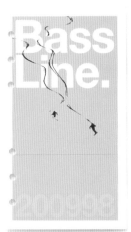

→05 *Bassline flyers, 1998 (Client: Paradiso)*

Move Your World presents

Bassline on Tour

1 | Doornroosje
Friday March 20 1998
The Show introducing Bassline
Live: Tasta Flava / the All-Star Breakers
DJ: KC the Funkaholic & Skelter
MC: Murth the Man-o-script / Shy-rock
Interactive Comedy: Freshwagon Crew
Open 22.00 Tickets 7,50 / After eleven 12,50

Groenewoudseweg 322 Nijmegen
024 3559887

2 | 't Paard
Sunday March 22 1998
Party Groove introducing Bassline
Live: Yukkie B. Wat Nou! / the Status
DJ: KC the Funkaholic, Rockid & Fanatic
MC: Murth / Brainpower
Interactive Comedy: Freshwagon Crew
Open 21.00 Tickets 15,- / In advance 10,-

Prinsengracht 12 Den Haag
070 3601838

3 | De Tagrijn
Friday March 27 1998
Masters of R-n-B introducing Bassline
Live: Yukkie B. Wat Nou! / the Lads
DJ: KC the Funkaholic & DJ Bartje
MC: Murth the Man-o-script
Interactive Comedy: Freshwagon Crew
Open 22.00 Tickets 15,- / In advance 12,50

Koninginneweg 44 Hilversum
035 6215841

Hiphop, R-n-B and Live Action.

   Paradiso
Produktiehuis

Bassline on Tour poster, 1998 (Client: Paradiso)

EXPERIMENTAL JETSET

"BassLife/LazyWife/BuckKnife/HighFive"—layered on top of evocative photographs with tenuous connections.

They also began to explore the use of color in ways that draw attention to the printed object primarily through overprinting one color on another and using the white of the paper as a third color. (White always existed in their design but had not been used to this degree of impact.)

By the time the studio stopped working on Paradiso in 1999, so that they could focus on design for other areas, they had laid the framework for the iconic work that would come over the next ten years, defined by a bold elemental typography, an emphasis on the materiality of graphic design, and an open-ended play of language and visual form.

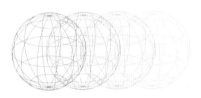

**Tomorrows
Sound Today.**
Drum-n-Bassline.

**Introducing
Drum-n-Bassline.
The Sound That Can
Shatter Glass.**

"Bam! Shattered Glass."

**Quite a claim.
Quite a sound.**
Drum-n-Bassline.

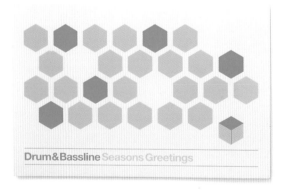

Drum&Bassline Seasons Greetings

Drum-n-Bassline flyers, 1997–99 (Client: Paradiso)

Bassline poster, 1998 (Client: Paradiso)

Paradisco poster, 1996 (Client: Paradiso)

Paradisco New Years Eve poster, 1998 (Client: Paradiso)

GRAPHIC THOUGHT FACILITY

The now familiar, and often overused, phrase "form follows function" finds resonance in the design of Graphic Thought Facility (GTF), though they use the word *function* loosely. GTF looks for formal solutions—a marriage of type, image, and materials, in their case—to the proposed problem of any given brief. Take, for example, a moving announcement and logo (1996) for Mighty, a production house. →01 The type is made of the gold stickers commonly used on mailboxes and DIY signage, with the *i* replaced with a directional arrow. While it is just a postcard and not the kind of ambitious identity system the studio is known for, it demonstrates in miniature the thinking behind their works.

GTF's book and poster design (both designed in collaboration with Peter Saville) for the exhibition Pop Art Is… (Gagosian Gallery, London, 2007) is anchored by British Pop artist Richard Hamilton's 1957 definition of pop art: "Popular, Transient, Expendable, Low cost, Mass produced, Young, Witty, Sexy, Gimmicky, Glamorous, Big business." →02 This list is set as a Brutalist statement in Helvetica Bold and used as the cover "image." It may appear similar to many of the new Modernist works being produced today, especially with its embossed cover, but GTF's typography is not International Typographic Style in nature, it is the graphic language of the generic— the signage of public restrooms, parking lots, corporations with forgettable names. In short, it is popular, transient, expendable, mass produced…

GTF's approach is so systems-oriented that their publication designs tend to be radically different from one to the next, unlike many book designers who have a general and recognizable sensibility apparent in each project. The Pop Is… catalog has a super stripped down cover and remains that way throughout. Compare this to the design of *Elizabeth Peyton: Live Forever* by Laura Hoptman (2009), a more traditionally beautiful book, yet one that reimagines the traditional structure of a book. →03 The content

→01 *Mighty logo, 1996 (Client: Mighty)*

Popular
Transient
Expendable
Low cost
Mass produced
Young
Witty
Sexy
Gimmicky
Glamorous
Big business

Pop Art is:
September 27–November 10, 2007
Britannia Street, London

Gagosian

GRAPHIC THOUGHT FACILITY

begins with the acknowledgments and table of contents on the inside front cover and a bold title page printed directly on the exposed text block. The book then dives straight into the content with some 225 pages of images before any more text appears. The three different sections of the book—reference material, the artist's work, and the commentary—are denoted simply by shifting paper stocks. The end result is a traditional-looking book with a radically different physicality.

The book *I Am A Camera* by The Saatchi Gallery (2000) plays with the tension of typography and structure in a similar fashion. →04 The captioning system, title page, table of contents, and essay are imagined as independent ideas, unrelated to each other, and is distributed seemingly at random throughout. This becomes a structural device for organizing the book and for highlighting the "real" content—in this case, the photography. The artwork is divided into three sections and begins immediately on the front cover. The other parts of the book—front matter and essay—are printed on a heavier stock so that they function as physical and conceptual dividers. These pages of heavier stock were inserted into the book's binding as tip-ins, which answered a practical concern—the need to continually update the sequence of the photos based on client feedback and to add new content throughout the process. By separating the dividers from the signatures of the book, reordering of the photography was possible as long as the overall page count didn't change.

GTF regularly confronts ideas about form and format. Because their solutions are so often rooted in the materiality of the piece, their typography is able to remain very traditional without appearing staid. Their radicalism lies deeper than the decision of what to do with the alphabet.

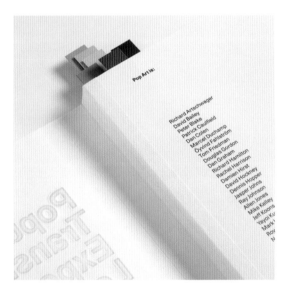

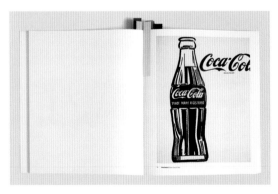

→02 Pop Art Is… *book, 2007 (Designed with Peter Saville; Client: Gagosian Gallery)*

→03 Live Forever: Elizabeth Peyton *book, 2009*
(Author: Laura Hoptman; Client: Phaidon)

GRAPHIC THOUGHT FACILITY

2
Tierney Gearon
Untitled
2000
C-print
122 × 183cm. / 48 × 72in.

→04 I Am A Camera *book, 2001 (Client: The Saatchi Gallery)*

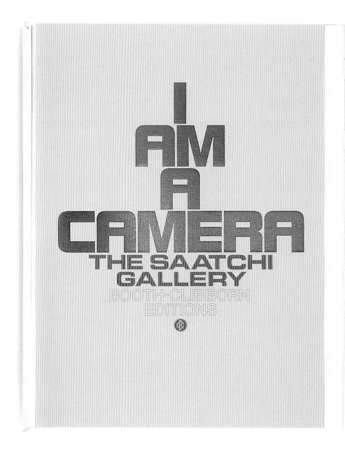

HEY HO

The French studio Hey Ho creates some of the most spare graphic design today. The residue of the most severe type of Swiss Typography—sans-serif type, an emphasis on structure, and a lack of ornamentation—lingers in their work, but not in a reverential or allegiant way. Whereas some designers practice a typographic dogmatism in which you see their influences clearly, Hey Ho use this influence toward one end—clarity.

In a rare turn, the designers of Hey Ho, Julien Hourcade and Thomas Petitjean, create work that is almost exclusively typographic, avoiding puns, references, or illustrations. Typography is the beginning and the end, and they pursue it relentlessly.

Since 2005 they have been the designers for French publisher Galaade Éditions, and their works are a testament to what can be accomplished with only the barest essentials of typography—one typeface, traditional grids, and black ink. *Mon Heure Sur La Terre* (My time on earth, 2008) by poet Claude Vigée is a study in extreme contrasts of graphic elements. →01 Underneath the dust jacket, the front and back covers are adorned with his initials *V* and *C*, respectively, and the chapter headings are set in all-caps type so large that it takes eight pages to display the first essay title. (This kind of Brutalism recurs in their body of work but is not the full extent of their interests.) The twelve-column grid used in *Mon Heure* allows for a great deal of fluctuation in column widths—from the simple essay pages to the highly involved table of contents, the most complex visualization of their grid. Multiple font weights and sizes are used to create an extremely clear and nuanced piece of information design. It is also situated on page 912—subverting the traditional reading of the book—and as if the complexity of the content increases from the beginning to the end. If the table of contents is not where one expects it to be, it would seem to indicate that this is a book about searching and starting anywhere.

→01 Mon Heure Sur La Terre *(My time on earth) book, 2008 (Author: Claude Vigée; Client: Galaade Éditions)*

HEY HO

Mon Heure, like much of Hey Ho's work for Galaade Éditions, uses extremely thin papers, which allow the other side to show through. Like Experimental Jetset, they are acutely aware of the printed matter as object and work to heighten the experience of it, whether by using the weight of the paper to reveal the grid and structure or by flooding the backsides of posters with a single color. They don't just consider the printed piece as a two-dimensional plane but as three-dimensional object with a front and a backside experienced in space.

The cultural journal *Particules* (Particles), which the firm has designed since 2006, displays much of the tendencies present in their other works. →02 But whereas Hey Ho uses white space to allow for visual ease in the Galaade projects, they employ thick black type densely set on text-heavy broadsheets for *Particules*. In the rare instance that a column isn't completely filled with text, the show through of the newsprint eliminates any sense of emptiness. Even with the visual heaviness of the individual pages, the overall high-contrast typography still maintains the clarity that marks their design.

The work of Hey Ho is a rare thing—few designers work exclusively in typography, and fewer still embark on such an elemental path where influences aren't readily apparent. But the outcome is a singular body of work with a purity of vision that actually proves to be timeless.

→02 Particules *(Particles) newspaper, 2006 (Client: Particules)* above back cover opposite front cover

PARTICULES N° 17   RÉFLEXIONS SUR L'ART ACTUEL

SOMMAIRE

N° 17

ONT PARTICIPÉ À CE NUMÉRO : CLARA SCHULMANN /
VINCENT LABAUME / MATHILDE VILLENEUVE /
ALAIN BERLAND / ELÉONORE DE SAINTAGNAN /
NICOLAS BOUYSSI / MARIE MAERTENS / YVES BROCHARD /
CATHERINE LAUBIER / BRUNO PERRAMANT /
CORINNE BERLAND / PHILIPPE MAYAUX / DIDIER VIVIEN/
GUILLAUME LEINGRE / VALÉRIE DA COSTA /
STÉPHANE CORRÉARD / DELPHINE GOATER /
SANDRINE NICOLAS.

MERCI À CEUX QUI, QUOI QU'ILS FASSENT, NOUS AIDENT...

PARTICULES 70 RUE DES PANOYAUX 75020 PARIS
DIRECTEUR DE LA PUBLICATION : GAËL CHARBAU
DESIGN : THOMAS PETITJEAN & JULIEN HOURCADE
(WWW.WEARETPJH.COM)
COMITÉ DE RÉDACTION : G. CHARBAU, A. BERLAND,
N. BOUYSSI, S. CORRÉARD
INTERNET : HTTP://JOURNALPARTICULES.FREE.FR
CONTACT : JOURNALPARTICULES@FREE.FR

IMPRIMÉ PAR : POLICROM / ISSN : 1763-7430
DÉPÔT LÉGAL : DÉCEMBRE 2006 / TIRAGE : 5000 EX.

VOUS SOUHAITEZ VOUS ABONNER À 6 NUMÉROS (1AN)
DU JOURNAL PARTICULES ?
DÉCOUPEZ ET COMPLÉTEZ LE COUPON CI-DESSOUS,
RETOURNEZ-LE À :
PARTICULES, 70 RUE DES PANOYAUX 75020 PARIS
ACCOMPAGNÉ D'UN CHÈQUE DE 20 EUROS
LIBELLÉ À L'ORDRE DES AMIS DU JOURNAL PARTICULES.

NOM

PRÉNOM

ADRESSE

CODE POSTAL

VILLE

E-MAIL

ÉDITORIAL

Pour que soit accordée plus d'attention à des artistes que nous jugeons importants, nous émettons, dans *Particules*, des propositions, des hypothèses, des projections.

Qu'on puisse regarder cette entreprise comme une guerre de territoire est sans doute inévitable. Mais de là à perdre son sang-froid... Sous l'énigmatique signature d'« Art press », la revue éponyme s'est livrée à une véritable « exécution » de notre contributeur Guy Scarpetta, avec une violence et un manque d'humour regrettables. Au juste, de quoi s'agissait-il ? D'une simple opposition entre deux choix dans l'art d'aujourd'hui. Corpet, Desgranchamps, Dufour, Pencréach, Tatah sont les « favourite things » de Richard Leydier, Scarpetta préfère pour sa part, Boudier, Jacquet, Labelle-Rojoux, Lavier, Mayaux ou Ramette... La belle affaire... Y a-t-il de quoi en venir aux mains ? Doit-on pour autant confondre débat d'idées et attaques personnelles ? C'est la grandeur de la condition de critique d'art que de se donner les moyens littéraires de ses engagements ; au temps de trier cruellement le bon grain de l'ivraie.

Pendant ce temps, les affaires continuent... Soumis à la contamination croisée des magnats de la bourse et des célébrités de la mode, le toujours infantile marché de l'art a attrapé une bonne varicelle : accès de fièvre et multiplication des points rouges ont encore été observés à la FIAC (in et off confondus). Les investisseurs spéculent, et les camelots du luxe s'offrent au passage une image d'avant-garde ; chacun reste dans son rôle, après tout. Mais qu'en pensent ceux, artistes, galeristes, critiques, conservateurs qui s'intéressent à l'art pour sa puissance de transformation du monde, non pour ces potentielles prises de bénéfices symboliques ou financières ?

À nos yeux, l'attribution du Prix Marcel-Duchamp à Philippe Mayaux est une divine surprise. Du coup, parmi les serviteurs zélés de la plus-value, certains se révèlent mauvais perdants et pleurnichent : « Encore une occasion de perdue pour la promotion de l'art français à l'international »...

Et pourtant, il suffit de feuilleter son catalogue raisonné pour constater que le succès actuel de Mayaux s'appuie sur un réseau de vrais amoureux, galeristes et collectionneurs français et étrangers, critiques et conservateurs, tous fervents défenseurs de cette œuvre dans sa durée, avec fidélité et engagement. La victoire des petits porteurs sur les gros investisseurs, en somme !

Est-ce une coïncidence ? Parmi ces défenseurs on trouve notamment Jean-Yves Jouannais, Didier Ottinger et Marc-Olivier Wahler. Les deux premiers ont été récemment choisis pour élaborer la prochaine Triennale du Grand-Palais, et le troisième dirige le Palais de Tokyo ; ils ont en commun d'être des artisans, des amoureux de l'art et des artistes qui se placent – les expositions inaugurales du nouveau Palais de Tokyo l'expriment avec brio – au service des œuvres. *Ils songent à l'art avec l'intention d'en être bouleversés*, comme disait Bernard Lamarche-Vadel.

Alors oui, certes, on aura remarqué que Mayaux n'était pas de « Notre Histoire », ni de « La Force de l'Art », il n'est peut-être pas encore dans la collection Pinault ; il n'a décidément rien en commun avec la « Start Up » Abdessemed... Non, Mayaux c'est plutôt un pôle d'innovations en nanotechnologies, pour filer la métaphore...

Son prix exprime le retour du refoulement des trop nombreux artistes qu'on a laissé passer, parce qu'on n'avait pas le temps, à force de vouloir coller aux tendances volatiles du marché international, de se pencher vraiment sur leur travail ; parce qu'on a toujours un problème avec notre passé et notre culture encombrante, et toujours un peu honte aussi face aux grosses machines de la concurrence mondiale, d'affirmer un tant soit peu de différence, d'étrangeté, ou de complexité.

PAR GAËL CHARBAU

EN COUVERTURE : THIERRY MOUILLÉ, *LIGHT BOX*, 2006.
IMPRESSION TRANSLUCENT ET BOÎTE LUMINEUSE, 80 X 100 CM.
COURTESY GALERIE CLAUDINE PAPILLON, PARIS.

Colectiv *(Collective) exhibition catalog, 2008 (Client: Arc en Rêve Centre d'Architecture)*

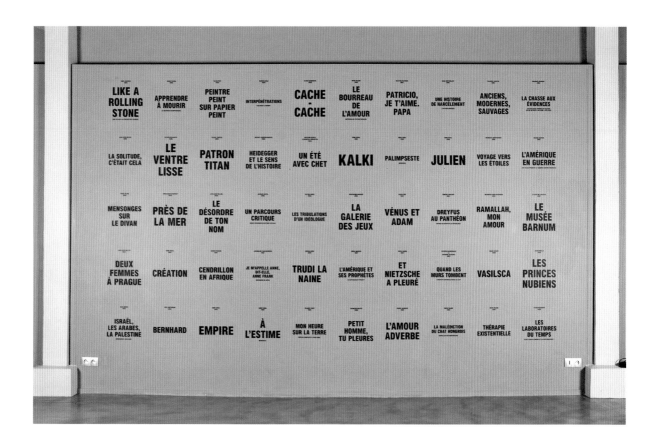

Interior graphics for Galaade Éditions office, 2008 (Client: Galaade Éditions)

Galaade Éditions *brochure, 2009 (Client: Galaade Éditions)*

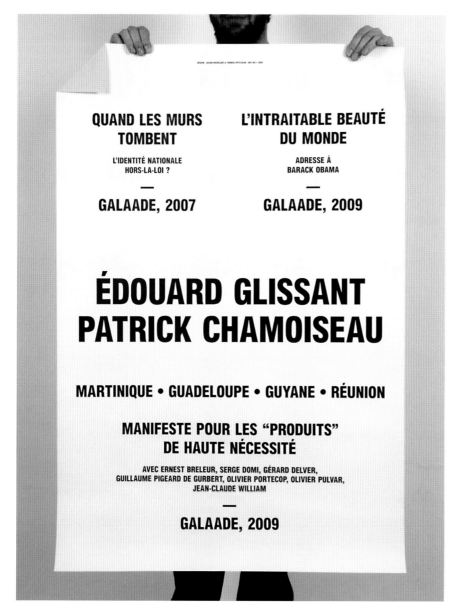

left *Galaade Éditions poster, 2009 (Client: Galaade Éditions)*

top right L'empreinte et le Tremblement *(The footprint and the trembling) book, 2009 (Author: Alain Fleischer; Client: Galaade Éditions)*

bottom right Manifeste pour les "Produits" de Haute Nécessité *(Manifesto for "products" of great necessity) pamphlet, 2009 (Authors: Édouard Glissant and Patrick Chamoiseau; Client: Galaade Éditions)*

HUDSON-POWELL

Hudson-Powell, the partnership of two brothers, Luke Powell and Jody Hudson-Powell, occupies a truly unique place in contemporary design practice: they are known equally for elegant print designs crafted for restaurants, cultural institutions, and fashion as they are for generative digital artworks and applications. Considering the wide chasm between these two practices, it is no surprise that the studio does a little of everything in-between as well.

They have received considerable acclaim for their digital projects, such as a custom piece of software that generates artwork to be used in the print promotions for the Barbican Theatre in London (2006) or their installation *Hello Kitty's Wizard Mirror* (Hong Kong International Trade and Exhibition Centre, Hong Kong, 2006), a fun-house-mirror-like project where viewers can see themselves with an ever-changing abstract head. But little has been discussed about their print work, which seems to have come from a completely different source. Their work for Canteen, a British restaurant in London, celebrates British design with references to the Classical typography of fifties Penguin book covers and the iconography of heraldic shields. The exterior signage set in Johnston Light (a precursor to Gill Sans) is a thing of beauty that exudes a timeless feel; the menus, placemats, and promotional materials are elegantly Modernist—serif type organized in a grid of ruled lines and white space. →01 This aesthetic is a shocking contrast to the neon colors and explosive imagery that is present in much of their digital work.

In projects like the fashion newsletter *Letters from London* (2008) and a record sleeve for the band Men-An-Tol (designed in collaboration with Jethro Haynes, 2006), a similar tension between Modernism and Traditionalism is at play. →02 & 03 Both designs luxuriate in their deep blacks while making use of a bold, Modern composition, but the use of humanist sans-serif typefaces softens the effect. Instead of appearing technical, the design evokes some other

Canteen invites you to celebrate our opening
November 29th 2005 *7pm–10pm*
RSVP Lisa Ispani *lisai@meenakhera.com*
020 7034 0200 A feasting buffet will be served throughout the evening

→01 *Canteen identity system, 2005 (Client: Canteen)* above ***opening invitation*** opposite top ***menu*** opposite bottom left ***signage***

Canteen is committed to providing honest food, nationally sourced, skillfully prepared and reasonably priced. We believe in good produce provenance. Our meat is additive free sourced directly from producers

CANTEEN

COOKED IN THE KITCHEN

JUST A REMINDER, UNLIKE MANY OF OUR CONTEMPORARIES WE DON'T USE FROZEN CHIPS, WE MAKE OUR OWN PIES, PICCALILLI, MARMALADE, ALL OUR CAKES AND ICE-CREAM, EVEN OUR JAMS ARE HOME-MADE. QUITE SIMPLY THEY TASTE BETTER THAT WAY.

Spread from Great British Food *brochure, 2008 (Client: Canteen)*

time in history—one that we don't know firsthand but are sure exists. The Powell brothers, like designer Peter Saville, especially in his early work, are masters of creating designs that unite contradictory themes, and conflicting times and places. It is for this reason that the work is so striking.

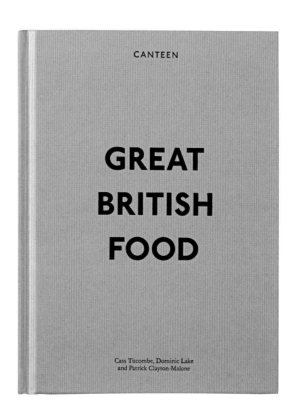

CANTEEN

GREAT BRITISH FOOD

Cass Titcombe, Dominic Lake
and Patrick Clayton-Malone

Canteen: Great British Food cookbook, 2010 (Authors: Cass Titcombe, Patrick Clayton-Malone, and Dominic Lake; Client: Ebury Press)

76

CURRIED PARSNIP SOUP
Serves 4

One of the best things we British learned when we used to rule the world was the use of heat in recipes. All of us at Canteen love curry and other spicy food, and this soup is a favourite with us as well as our customers.

25ML SUNFLOWER OIL
500G PARSNIPS, CHOPPED
1 MEDIUM ONION, CHOPPED
100G CELERIAC, CHOPPED
100G LEEKS, CHOPPED
4 GARLIC CLOVES, CRUSHED
3CM PIECE FRESH ROOT GINGER, GRATED
1 TBSP CURRY POWDER
1/2 TSP GROUND TURMERIC
1/2 TSP FENNEL SEEDS
1/2 TSP CORIANDER SEEDS
1 LITRE VEGETABLE STOCK (SEE P202, NOTE)
1 BUNCH SPRING ONIONS, SHREDDED
JUICE OF 1 LEMON
SALT AND BLACK PEPPER

1. Heat up the sunflower oil in a large saucepan. Add the parsnips, onion, celeriac and leeks and sweat for about 10 minutes or until soft but not brown. 2. Add the garlic, ginger and spices. Cook for 5 more minutes, stirring occasionally. 3. Add the stock and some salt and and bring to the boil. Add the spring onions and simmer for 30–40 minutes until all the vegetables are tender. 4. Blend until smooth. Add the lemon juice and check the seasoning. If the soup is too thick, add more stock or some water. Reheat before serving, if necessary.

PEA AND HAM SOUP
Serves 6–8

The English tradition of boiled salt pork and pease pudding is the inspiration for this soup. It is hearty and warming, which is just what you need when you feel that damp wintry chill in your bones.

1 LARGE ONION, ROUGHLY CHOPPED
150G CELERY (ABOUT 6 STICKS), INCLUDING LEAVES, CUT IN CHUNKS
150G LEEKS, CHOPPED
4 GARLIC CLOVES, CHOPPED
2 LITRES GAMMON STOCK (P84)
200G DRIED SPLIT PEAS
SMALL HANDFUL OF PARSLEY STALKS, IF YOU HAVE THEM
100G GAMMON TRIMMINGS
10G FRESH CHIVES, SNIPPED
BLACK PEPPER

1. Put the onion, celery, leeks and garlic into a saucepan. Add the stock, split peas and parsley stalks. 2. Bring to the boil, then simmer for 1–1½ hours until the peas are soft. 3. Remove from the heat and allow to cool for 30 minutes. Blend until smooth, then pass through a fine sieve. 4. Chop the gammon trimmings. Stir into the soup with the chives. If it is too thick, add some water. Season with black pepper. Reheat and serve hot.

NOTES: You should not need to add any salt to this soup because the gammon stock will be salty • If you don't have any gammon stock, or gammon trimmings, you can make this soup with Chicken or Meat stock (p202) and add some chopped cooked ham.

HUDSON-POWELL

→02 Letters from London *newsletter, 2008 (Client: London Fashion Week)*

→03 Men-An-Tol *CD, 2006 (Designed with Jethro Haynes; Artist/Client: Men-An-Tol)*

HUDSON-POWELL

2008

CONCRETE AND GLASS

WELCOME TO CONCRETE & GLASS 2008

This years curators Flora Fairbairn and Tom Baker and the backroom team behind Concrete and Glass have been working hard these past months to bring you a new, interesting and varied event for East London that we hope will entertain and inspire you.

The whole idea of a music and art event we know sounds a bit stuffy, but basically what we hope we do is expose you to a bunch of stuff that you wouldn't ordinarily see.

Music artists playing across the two days include Stockholm's sultry popster Lykke Li, experimental Brooklyn legends TV on the Radio, who play their first show on these shores for nearly two years.

Reading's Pete and The Pirates, electronic heroes Fujiya and Miyagi, and James Holden, an amazing Wire magazine line up, industry buzz band's Twisted Wheel and Flashguns and many more appear. There are also a couple of less straight forward shows on offer; we welcome Italian minimal modern composer Ludovico Einaudi who has a Steinway piano booked, tuned and ready for his show at Cargo on Thursday; you might not know him but he wrote the beautiful film score to Shane Meadow's 'This Is England' (2006). Another must see has to be accordionist Kimmo Pohjonen, whose show at Cafe 1001 will feature live actual farmers! accompanying him on their agricultural equipment!

Alongside the amazing music line ups that take place in East London's tried and tested venues, there are over 20 specially commissioned art exhibitions that are scattered around the area; these range from shop windows becoming gallery spaces, Arnold Circus' bandstand being turned into a seismic sound exhibition by Measure, a DJ stand off at Whitechapel Gallery involving kung fu (?!) and David Blandy, a specially commission

ART
All venues are subject to capacity and all times relate to 2nd & 3rd of October.

Concrete & Glass Presents:
HEART OF GLASS
curated by Flora Fairbairn & Paul Hitchman
2 October–19 October — *Basement, Shoreditch Town Hall,*
6.30pm–10pm — *380 Old Street EC1V 9LT*
Heart of Glass, a show of new, site-specific work by 25 established and emerging artists in Shoreditch Town Hall's basement, is the hub of the arts projects. The Artists have been selected by open-submission – a panel of art-world luminaries including Marc Quinn, Gavin York, Rachel Campbell-Johnston (Art critic), Paul Hudson (Contemporary Art Society), Irene Bradbury (Associate Director, White Cube) and Philippa Adams (Saatchi Gallery) will select the most interesting work to show with the artist winning a solo show in CONCRETE & GLASS next year.

Artprojx Presents:
DAVID BLANDY: DUELS AND DUALITIES
3rd October — *Whitechapel Gallery, 80–82*
6.30pm–10pm — *Whitechapel High St E1 7QX*
An examination of the quest for the authentic and the spiritual in the ephemeral world of popular culture. Can you ever find the self in the other? The battle is a fundamental aspect of many underground cultural movements- the MC battle, the one on one beat-em-up, cutting heads in a blues guitar duel, or turntablist vs. turntablist. The Artprojx Dojo will explore these legacies, and how the idea of a quest for perfection is pursued through them. Bringing together an array of underground artistic forms, Kung fu and Chanbara flicks, hardcore fighting arcade games, comics and a dub sound system, Blandy continues his quest for identity.

Barclays Capital Presents:
ITHAKA
by Alexander Hedison
2 October–19 October — *Ground Floor, Shoreditch Town*
6.30pm–10pm — *Hall, 380 Old Street EC1V 9LT*
Structured around journeys, Hedison's work addresses themes of loss, transition, and recovery as photographs in various locations around the world searching for each site's complex identity. Using the temporate rainforest of the Pacific Northwest as an illustration of the internal odyssey that comes with change, Hedison formed the body of work titled ITHAKA, inspired by C.P. Cavafy's poem of the same name. In the poem Cavafy begins by offering a piece of advice: "As you set out for Ithaka, pray that the road is a long one, full of adventure, full of discovery." For Hedison, this series of photographs is not a literal portrayal of the forest but rather an attempt to chart and in fact document the process of personal growth. Using the forest as a metaphor, Hedison's work illustrates the journey from a recognisable place to one that is unfamiliar, in fact presenting the individuals journey through life itself.

Catherine Lorca Presents:
MAKE BELIEVE
3 October–19 October — *Nichols & Clarke, 3–10*
6.30pm–10pm — *Shoreditch High Street, E1 6PE*
If Art concerns the manifestation of an idea through the handling of material, this exhibition presents a renewed emphasis on the productive gap between practice and product. Tyce track, icing sugar, feather, lard, wood, plaster, paint, paper, porcelain, video and photography- in a seductive array of media, this show highlights the artwork's passage from base materiality to symbolic form. From Ruth Claxton's adapted 'found' postcards to Boo Ritson's photographs of thickly painted people, adopting subject matter ranging from classical mythology to the effect of the internet on our sense of orientation. Artists: Jodie Carey, Ruth Claxton, Katarina Fritz, Nick Hornby, Ryan Mosley, Daniel Pasteiner, Boo Ritson, Ceal Warnants

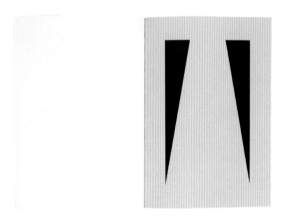

The Gainsborough Packet, &c *book, 2009 (Author: Matt Stokes;*
Client: 176 / Zabludowicz Collection)

HUDSON-POWELL

*Centre for Fashion Enterprise poster, 2008 (Designed with Zak Kyes;
Client: Centre for Fashion Enterprise)* above *front* opposite *back*

CENTRE FOR FASHION ENTERPRISE

The CFE is a pioneering business incubator that supports new, existing and sustainable fashion businesses.

Fashion is a tough business. All too often the talent, passion and drive of some of London's best new designers can go unnoticed and unrewarded. At the CFE we have made it our aim to assist selected designers by providing an innovative support platform of business services; grant schemes, studio space and strategic advice that supports and complements the creative talents of each designer.

The CFE is principally funded and supported by London Development Agency and London College of Fashion.

London College of Fashion's support of fashion design talent continues to build international reputations and business growth.

contact the CFE
enquiries@fashion-enterprise.com
182 Mare Street
London E8 3RE
Tel +44 (0) 207 7514 7659

visit the CFE
www.fashion-enterprise.com

Previously Supported
Basso and Brooke
Charlott Vasberg
Julia Clancey
Maresh Arora
Yoko Yoshitake

Creative Direction
Rafael Jimenez

Graphic Design
Hudson-Powell, Zak Group

MODERNIST

"sophistication sewn into every seam" — Sarah Mower

SALES: For sales appointments contact Fiona at easternBlock
Tel +44 (0) 207 105 2727
Fax +44 (0) 207 435 2726
sales@easternblock.co.uk
Paris Showroom
23 Rue Du Renard
75004 Paris

PRESS: Blow PR
Tel +44 (0) 207 436 9449
Fax +44 (0) 207 436 7027
info@blow.co.uk
29-35 Rathbone Street
London W1T 1NJ

MARIOS SCHWAB

"Marios Schwab came out with the freshest surprise of the London shows: a collection that was not only precariously well made, but also stamped with an authentic, viewpoint. Marios Luca Promatico, of the influential Paris boutique Maria Luisa, left raving" — Sarah Mower

SALES: for sales appointments contact Maria at Rainbow Wave
Tel +44 (0) 207 352 0002
Fax +44 (0) 207 352 0005
info@rainbowwave.com

Paris Showroom
Galerie Artcore
40 Rue De Richelieu
75001 Paris
Tel +33 1 4703 0960
Fax +33 1 4703 0960

PRESS: AL
Tel +44 (0) 207 287 1314
Fax +44 (0) 207 287 1315
sclare@sage.co.uk
Unit 8.10 B Archer Street
London W1D 7AZ

ERDEM

On his design "Erdem is as much about the indispensable as the design" — Ian P. Webb

SALES: for sales appointments contact Maria at Rainbow Wave
Tel +44 (0) 207 352 0002
Fax +44 (0) 207 352 0005
info@rainbowwave.com

Paris Showroom
Galerie Artcore
40 Rue De Richelieu
75001 Paris
Tel +33 1 4703 0960
Fax +33 1 4703 0960

PRESS: Modus Publicity
Tel +44 (0) 7338 7482
Fax +44 (0) 7338 7444
sarah@moduspublicity.com

GAVIN DOUGLAS

"Douglas has the nostalgia of fifties print couture with Blade-runner future-world sexiness" — Ian P. Webb

SALES: For sales appointments contact Hongxi at Blow
Tel +44 (0) 207 436 9449
Fax +44 (0) 207 436 7027
h@blow.co.uk

London Showroom
29-35 Rathbone Street
London W1T 1NJ

PRESS: Blow PR
Tel +44 (0) 207 436 9449
Fax +44 (0) 207 436 7027
info@blow.co.uk
29-35 Rathbone Street
London W1T 1NJ

FASHION FRINGE

"As our chairman Tom Ford has said, Fashion Fringe is all about the celebration of individual creativity which is unique to London" — Colin McDowell

SALES: For sales queries please contact Caroline at 2MO
Tel +44 (0) 208 533 6588
fashionfringe@zingworld.com

PRESS: Nick Rogers at Maison
Tel +44 (0) 207 491 6680
+44 (0) 7736 670 816
nick@maison-media.co.uk

ZAK KYES

Zak Kyes has received a great deal of attention for his work as a recent graduate with a burgeoning design practice. What makes many of Kyes's projects so memorable is his ability to use the subject of a brief as a jumping point to create larger ideas that linger as conceptual works long after the piece has fulfilled its pragmatic purpose as an announcement.

His poster for the workshop Impunities: A Two Day Experiment in Writing and Community (REDCAT, Los Angeles, 2006) uses as its content a Google News search for the term *impunity* and adopts Google's HTML-oriented defaults as its visual basis. This strategy reflects the agenda of the workshop in a variety of ways: it becomes an experiment in writing by using a text that no one individual has control over and which was written by a community of authors located all over the world.

Kyes does not follow a stylistic agenda; rather, his works often reference an archetypal typography— by using HTML defaults for Impunities or by mimicking the typography of a novel for a poster for Oulipo (after Georges Perec) (2005), a conference on the sixties experimental writing group Oulipo. →01 The poster is treated in such a Brutalist manner that there is little mistaking that it is meant to look like a page of a book. Such projects also display a desire to turn something as simple as a promotional poster into a vehicle for developing content.

In 2005 Kyes relocated to London to take the position of art director for AA Print Studio, the group that fulfills all design and production needs for the Architectural Association (AA) in London. His work at the AA has allowed for an even greater engagement with content—in 2007 he curated Forms of Inquiry: the Architecture of Critical Graphic Design, a traveling exhibition for the AA, as well as working on multiple publications and posters. The exhibition and its catalog looked at the relationship between contemporary graphic design and architecture. →02 The AA created Bedford Press in 2008, a private

→01 *Oulipo (after Georges Perec) poster, 2005 (Reproduced in* The nOulipian Analects*; Client: self-published)*

→02 top *Forms of Inquiry: the Architecture of Critical Graphic Design exhibition, 2009 (Client: self-published)*

bottom row The nOulipian Analects *book, 2007 (Client: self-published)*

ZAK KYES

press operated by Kyes and AA Print Studio and in collaboration with Wayne Daly. In this role, Kyes has acted as editor on a number of publications, and in 2009 a new imprint, Bedford Press Editions, a series of artist's books edited by Kyes, was launched. These activities put Kyes more squarely in the role of content developer.

MANIFESTO PAMPHLET   18/19.10.08

A pamphlet for the Serpentine Gallery Manifesto Marathon 2008:

1. The historic avant-gardes of the early 20th century and the neo-avant-gardes in the 1960s and 70s created a time of radical manifestos.

2. We now live in a time that is more atomised and has less cohesive artistic movements.

3. At this moment, there is a reconnection to the manifesto as a document of poetic and political intent.

4. This is a declaration of artistic will and new-found optimism.

5. New modes of publication and production are a means to distribute ideas in the form of texts, documents, and radical pamphlets.

6. This futurological congress presents manifestos for the 21st century. This event is urgent.

Marathon Manifesto 2008 *pamphlet, 2008*
(Client: Serpentine Gallery)

Architectural Association
School of Architecture

AA Bar and Front Members' Room
Friday 19 September 2008

6.30–8.30pm

1968

Architectural Association
36 Bedford Square
London WC1B 3ES

RSVP:
cristian@aaschool.ac.uk
aaschool.net

On the evening of Friday 19 September
2008 the Architectural Association will
honour members who were students at
the AA School of Architecture in 1968.
Please join us on this occasion to meet
up with former classmates, many of
whom are now changing the face of
architecture in London and across the
world, and share your memories of an
era of unique energy and creativity.

Photo: AA Photo Library

1968 reception invitation, 2008 (Client: AA School of Architecture)

ZAK KYES

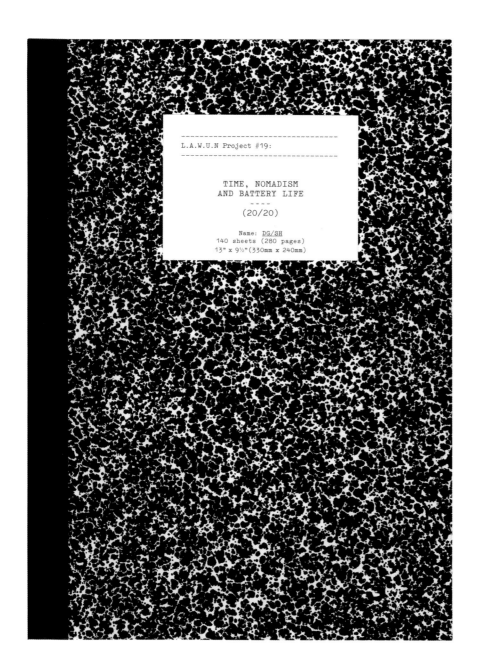

L.A.W.U.N Project #19 *book (Authors: David Greene and Samantha Hardingham;*
Client: AA School of Architecture)

SECTION 2: C72—107

THE ARCHITECTURE COMES TO YOU

ZAK KYES

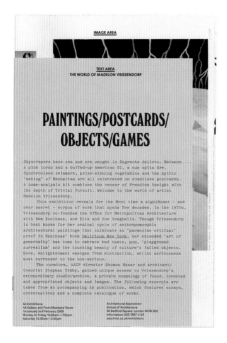

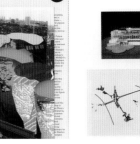

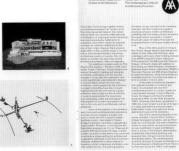

AA Gallery exhibition programs, 2007–9 (Client: AA School of Architecture)

GALLERY

PAINTINGS of metropolitan
zombies, a birthday party for
post-modern buildings, and naff
surrealist parodies form a body
of images where rooms become
backdrops for psychic-dramas
and scale constantly misbehaves.

'Despite her predilection for
"bad paintings" (a selection
of which are to be seen on the
facing wall), there is nothing
"bad" about Madelon's paintings,
drawings and etchings per se.
Quite the opposite. They are
technically and conceptually
complex; schematically worked
out and also left to be teased
by old-fashioned intuition.
Her images show trysts between
people and things that should
never really encounter each
other, and yet, when they do,
they generate an emotive effect
that pulls between beauty,
absurdity and hilarity. They
are, in her daughter Charlie's
words, "playground surrealism"
– that is, surreal without being
serious. "Sometimes the most
unserious things are the
funniest, and sometimes the
funniest things are the most
unserious", explains Madelon,
keeping a straight face.'

Shumon Basar

POSTCARDS dating from the late
19th century onwards are filed
in their thousands according to
highly specific categories. This
postcard archive discloses
unauthorised histories of
America, including the embers
of slavery, the original dreams
behind the Twin Towers and an
enduring fascination with
picket-fences.

'Madelon and Rem collected
thousands of postcards, as did
Eduardo Paolozzi, Richard
Hamilton and Alvin Boyarsky and
every 'knowing consumer'
educated in the hothouse of
London pop. Lectures of the
Independent Group during the
1950s established this form of
intellectual research. It
became the way to fashion an
alternative image-bank… "Maddie"
(as she is known for her mad-
insights and stream-of-
unconsciousness) had a postcard
of the lighthouse over Miami
Beach and she painted it above
the illicit bed [Flagrant
Délit]. Out come its pulsating
beams, picked out by the
moonbeams over the beach and
the car's intrusive headlights…
Postcards whispered to Maddie
"go there", and she did,
quite innocently.'

Charles Jencks

IMAGE AREA

ZAK KYES

Architectural Association
School of Architecture

Future Non-Future exhibits dozens
of contemporary urban, architectural
and landscape projects for London,
all of which share one main feature:
they remain unrealised.

Contributors:
Aran Architects
AOC
Avanti Architects
Cityscape
Daniel Libeskind
DRMM
FAT
DA
Foster + Partners
Future Systems
George Liapopoulos-Legendre
Grimshaw Architects
Hayes Davidson
Horden Cherry Lee
Ken Yeang
Lifschutz Davidson Sandilands
M3
Mark Guard Architects
MVRDV
MYAA
Nigel Coates
Nils Norman
NL Architects
OMA
Rogers Stirk Harbour + Partners
Sheppard Robson
Skylon
Squire and Partners
Studio 8 / CJ Lim
UN Studio
Ushida Findlay Architects
Wilkinson Eyre
Zaha Hadid

FUTURE NON-FUTURE

The Contemporary Unbuilt
Architecture of London

The Director of the AA School
of Architecture Brett Steele
invites you to a private view on
Friday 3 October 2008, 6.30–8.30pm

AA Gallery
6 to 29 October 2008
Monday to Friday 10am–7pm
Saturday 10am–3pm

Architectural Association
36 Bedford Square
London WC1B 3ES
Information 020 7887 4145
aaschool.net

Printed at Bedford Press, London / bedfordpress.org

Future Non-Future exhibition invitation, 2008 (Client: AA School of Architecture)

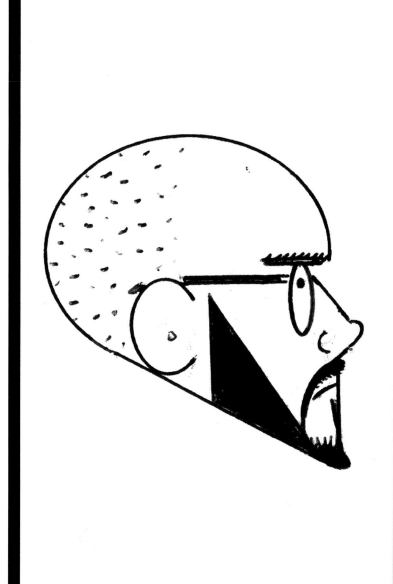

Lecture by Ryan Gander poster, 2007 (Illustration by Ed Fella; Client: AA School of Architecture)

ZAK KYES

THE

The Violence of Participation
Edited by Markus Miessen

Dear future participant of violent life on earth: If you are meant to be born as a human being then call yourself lucky if it's in Europe. Not too dry, not too cold, not too hot. No one has to starve or freeze and basic education is free. You can pretty much say and think what you want (please do not insult individuals) and at the same time vote without having to let anyone know about it. Women basically have the same rights as men. There are even public areas were it's totally fine to gather naked and swim or sweat - with hardly any danger of getting raped. Europe used to be the heart of Christianity, but now it's the last pagan outpost, maybe the first of its postindustrial kind - if not, the monotheists are reproducing too quickly. The European Union is constantly expanding Eastward, subsidizing new land and its inhabitants instead of conquering them. Meanwhile, the West is being devoured by a rising sea level, turning the original European lot into a South Sea archipelago, only with taxes. By not opting for expansion into Africa and Russia, the new Europe appears not to be imperialistic like the Roman Empire or the Third Reich. But just as Europe tries to make its membership less a burden than a gift and allows its countries to leave the Union at any time, any country from any part of the world that is, per se, not expected to join the European Union is expelled from it. In this way, Europe's behavior with regard to the rest of the world is dirty old apartheid. Europe's non-nationalistic democratism defeats the possibility of a democratic world government. Call it a paradox. Or call it another fortress of the rich. With lots of milk and little honey.

Yours,
Ingo Niermann

Sternberg Press

The Violence of Participation book, 2007 (Editor: Markus Miessen; Client: Sternberg Press)

The Violence of Participation
ISBN 978-1-933128-34-4

© 2007 Markus Miessen, Sternberg Press,
the authors. All rights reserved,
including the right of reproduction
in whole or in part in any form.

Publisher:
Sternberg Press

Editor:
Markus Miessen

Translator:
Gerrit Jackson

Copy editor:
Courtney Johnson

Design:
Zak Kyes, Zak Group
Design Assistant: Lina Maria Grumm
Sunbury Workshops, London
www.zakgroup.co.uk

Typeset in Stempel Schneidler designed
by F.H. Schneidler in 1936 for the
Bauer foundry. Stempel Schneidler
is based on early European typefaces
used by Venetian printers during the
Renaissance.

Printer:
Cassochrome, Belgium

Binder:
Binderij Hexspoor, Netherlands

Sternberg Press
Caroline Schneider
Karl-Marx-Allee 78, D-10243 Berlin
1182 Broadway #1602, New York NY 10001
mail@sternberg-press.com
www.sternberg-press.com

The editor would like to thank
the following people:

Negar Azimi, Ute Meta Bauer,
Christophe Beaudouin, Antonia Carver,
Celine Condorelli, Lisa Farjam,
Jesko Fezer, Anselm Franke,
Frédérique Gautier, Tatjana Günthner,
Ingeborg Harms, Mathias Heyden,
Nikolaus Hirsch, Gerrit Jackson,
Courtney Johnson, Oscar Kilawe,
Rem Koolhaas, Amanda Machin,
Stéphanie Moisdon, Chantal Mouffe,
Eva Munz, Molly Nesbit,
Michelle Nicol, Ingo Niermann,
Vincent Normand, Sean O'Toole,
Sunny Rahbar, Patricia Reed,
Karl Schlögel, Brett Steele and the
Architectural Association,
Stephan Trüby, Lorraine Two,
Srdjan Jovanovic Weiss, Eyal Weizman,
Tirdad Zolghadr, as well as all
participants of the drawing project,
both before and during the 2007 Lyon
Biennial.

Throughout the project, these people
have been a source of invaluable
motivation and support:

Shumon Basar, Erhard Eppler,
Hans Ulrich Obrist, Ralf Pflugfelder,
Nina Spreckelmeyer, and Zak Kyes.

The designer would like to thank
the following people:

Grégory Ambos, Laurence Soens,
Lina Maria Grumm, Radim Pesko,
Michaël Bussaer, Sara De Bondt,
and Susan Turcot.

This project would have been
impossible without the generous support
and belief of Caroline Schneider.

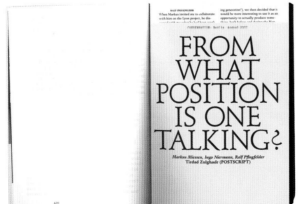

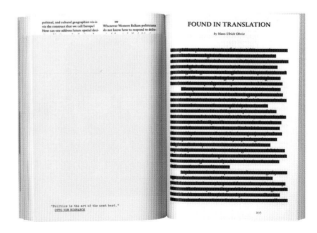

MANYSTUFF

French blogger Charlotte Cheetham started the design blog Manystuff in 2006 to share the graphic design work that interested her. Over the course of a few years, it became one of the most influential design blogs in the world, showcasing (and possibly kick-starting) many of the developments of the new century: the return of geometry, self-publishing, three-dimensional typography, and the new forms of Modernist and Minimalist design. Manystuff has recently branched into curating and publishing, with projects like the group show Reflet (Reflection, 2008) at Espace GHP in Toulouse, France; *Pressroom*, a daily publication created at the Work In Progress student exhibition (2009) at the Royal College of Art; and the *Manystuff* magazine.

What is your own educational and professional background? Do you see a relationship between that and your interest in graphic design? I studied communication and art history. I did internships related to contemporary art. I have always been immersed in the world of art: my grandfather and uncle were painters; my mother is a painting restorer and was an art dealer for a while. So, I have always been immersed in an "art world," which taught me at an early age how to look at and understand an image.

How did Manystuff begin? The story of Manystuff is a bit incidental: My boyfriend is a graphic designer, as are a lot of my friends. I started to research graphic designers on the Internet, because it was not a subject I was very familiar with. I loved what I discovered. I started the blog one day, and it went very well. More and more people were visiting and gradually it became a serious activity for me.

Were there certain qualities you were looking for in the work you were posting? Manystuff is a daily selection based on my personal graphic choices. I don't look for defined qualities. I am interested in creative and authorial graphic design; graphic designers who try to experiment; and those who say something through their work. I don't have formal criteria, though there is a certain consistency and aesthetic, but overall the coverage goes in waves. For example, right now I am very interested in small publishing initiatives, which are often related to a low-tech graphic design (typewriter, scan styles). This will probably change soon. Two years ago I was interested in graphic design related to "net art." My interests influence my internet research, and as a consequence the posts on Manystuff are related to that. Really, nothing more.

Manystuff seemed to champion a new kind of underground graphic design. Did you feel like the designers you were showcasing were doing something out of the ordinary? Yes, some of them really are innovators. Designers like Abäke, Karl Nawrot, Pierre Vanni, Harsh Patel, and so many more who are instigators of new research, are members of contemporary practices that try to answer their

MANYSTUFF

clients' briefs in unexpected ways, or initiate their
own publishing and exhibition projects. The Manystuff
selection isn't exhaustive. I try every day to show
what is interesting to me. Sometimes I'm struck by
the genius of some of the graphic designers shown
on Manystuff.

Did you notice a point at which the work
Manystuff was promoting began to influence graphic
design as a whole? Yes I know. I can't control that.
Manystuff can be a good or bad tool depending on
how it is used. I do Manystuff to show people—
graphic designers and nondesigners, students and
professionals—living anywhere in the world, what is
going on in graphic design. The idea is to encourage
meetings and discussions and to enlarge the vision
of people to something more than what they learned
in school or saw in their hometown. The misuse of
the blog would be to copy what is shown in thinking
that this is what is good.

Manystuff presents a small selection of what is
done. It's not exhaustive, and people should obviously
not reduce graphic design to what I present.

I was wondering about a more general influence—
I've actually heard people say, "the Manystuff look."
How do you feel about this? Do you feel like you've
helped to create or catalyze a movement? I'm not
sure that this is true. I don't see Manystuff to be
that important. I just think that a lot of people
react to the ideas proposed every day on the blog,
and that's great.

For example, in November I went to the Royal
College of Art in London. I was invited to report
on Manystuff at Work in Progress, an exhibition
of student projects. During this event the students
and I made a daily print publication.

A French graphic design student in a French
school was so impressed by what these students
were doing that he decided to start a project called
Parallel School in order to collaborate with
international students. I think that's very great.

You recently published the first issue of *Manystuff* magazine and curated exhibitions of graphic design. What led you to go into publishing and curatorial projects? I really think that the Internet has limits. It's not "real." I am attracted to tangible projects, to the idea of leaving traces, to meeting people, to real interaction. I think that's more interesting.

How did these projects come about? Were you approached by other people to start these projects, or did you go into them yourself? It depends. Some of the projects I had in mind already, like my first exhibition, Reflet. And sometimes they are unexpected projects, such as a special issue of the Korean publication *Graphic*—they contacted me to ask if I was interested.

What are you trying to accomplish with these initiatives? It depends on the project, but the idea with publishing or curatorial projects is to go further than the blog, to explore a theme or develop an overarching concept.

As Manystuff has branched into publishing and exhibitions, how do you see graphic design changing? I think that one of the fundamental changes is the increasing multidisciplinarity of the field of graphic design. The borders are becoming increasingly fuzzy, and there's a greater mixture of disciplines, with graphic design merging with photography, curating, writing, and illustrating. The voices of graphic designers are growing richer.

Whose work really interests you right now? www.manystuff.org is the answer to that. My choices and my projects make up the best answer to that question.

MGMT.

During a 2008 visit to the International Center for Photography (ICP) in New York City, I encountered an amazing piece of design. The title wall for Archive Fever: Uses of the Document in Contemporary Art exhibit was a floor-to-ceiling installation of every participant's name set in black Akzidenz Grotesk on a dark gray two-story wall. →01 No visual references to the idea of documents—typewritten text, form letters, paperclips or folders—were present. Instead, Akzidenz Grotesk was used as a serious indicator of "un-design," in much the same way that Daniel Eatock used it in his template projects or Müller-Brockmann on the cover of his *The Graphic Artist and His Design Problems* (1961). A similar tonal use of Akzidenz was present on a book that seemed omnipresent at that time, Bill Addis's *Building: 3000 Years of Design, Engineering and Construction* (2007). →02 It was bolder, more textural and colorful than Archive Fever but seemed to indicate a similar respect for Swiss Typography of the sixties. I later discovered that both were designed by the New York City–based studio MGMT.

Their book designs display a soft approach, within a limited range of tones, to information graphics and organization. Clarity is a concern, and fetishized informational gestures, like overuse of rule lines, tiny decorative type, or unnecessary keys, are absent. The use of the grid as a planar structure is what makes their work contemporary. Raul A. Barrenche's *Modern House Three* (2005), a collection of recent domestic architecture, clearly echoes the graphic design of architectural books of the sixties, with its use of all lower-case Helvetica, three-column grid, and limited color palette. →03 But it also takes advantage of the ease with which a column of type can be separated from its background when placed in a text box of a different color—a gesture that would have been costly and inefficient in the predigital era and one that is used throughout their work.

→01 *Archive Fever: Uses of the Document in Contemporary Art exhibition title wall, 2008 (Client: International Center for Photography)*

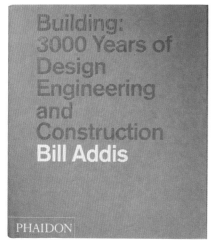

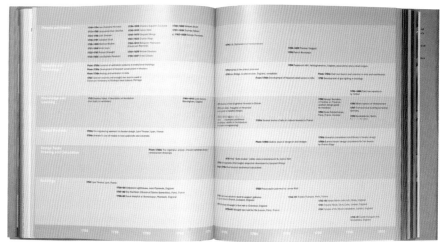

→02 Building: 3000 Years of Design, Engineering and Construction *book, 2007*
(Author: Bill Addis; Client: Phaidon)

MGMT.

In a series of books for the Yale School of Architecture, a forward-looking scientific aesthetic is created by giving the text columns semitransparent backgrounds and laying them over building renderings. →04 The same formal elements present in projects like *Building* or *Modern House Three*—Akzidenz Grotesk, restricted color schemes, minimal page designs—are also apparent in these books, but simple gestures like all-caps typesetting, a stricter use of black and white, and full-bleed photography make for a vastly different experience.

In the works intended for mainstream audiences, like Al Gore's *An Inconvenient Truth: The Planetary Emergency of Global Warming and What We Can Do About It* (2006), MGMT. →05 surprises with a lighter tone that still shows a great deal of respect for the reader's intelligence through its use of a spacious and clean design more reminiscent of art photography books than a primer on environmental issues. In the design culture of the United States, restraint and order are often used only when "appropriate" to the context of a project, meaning that design is supposed to look a certain way based on the expectations of the audience—a kind of demented spin on the "form follows function" principle. MGMT.'s work is refreshing for its emphasis on clarity and order as a point of view, not a sales point.

→03 Modern House Three *book, 2005*
(Author: Raul A. Barreneche; Client: Phaidon)

MGMT.

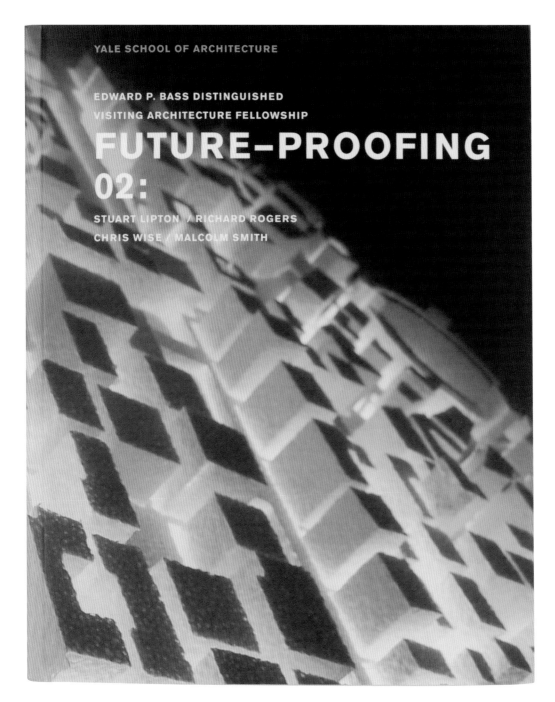

Inside the image:

YALE SCHOOL OF ARCHITECTURE

EDWARD P. BASS DISTINGUISHED
VISITING ARCHITECTURE FELLOWSHIP
FUTURE–PROOFING
02:

STUART LIPTON / RICHARD ROGERS
CHRIS WISE / MALCOLM SMITH

→04 Future-Proofing 02: Stuart Lipton/Richard Rogers/Chris Wise/Malcolm Smith *book, 2007*
(Author/Client: Yale School of Architecture)

The Neighborhoop is a series of paired towers that are linked at the base and the top. Each pair can be developed separately and consists of roughly 300 units. The design provides light, air, views, and private terraces for each unit.

Russell Greenberg and Adam Ganser "The Neighborhoop" developed out of a fear of the ordinary. It is a direct response to the Stratford City proposal by Arup, which numbs the economic, physical, and cultural conflicts inherent in the site with familiar, painfully buildable urban scenarios. While the Arup plan fulfills its technical obligations to existing local infrastructure and capitalizes on global connections via the Channel Tunnel Rail Link, it fails to even attempt an image for Stratford City that registers the extraordinary circumstances of these foreign/domestic alliances. We propose that the future appeal of Stratford City is more secure as a bizarre spatial offspring of unlikely parents than as a normative development without a trace of its origins.

The Neighborhoop is a mutant icon: part Eiffel Tower, part Stonehenge, part home. It stands as a monument to the vague status of public space in a private development like Stratford City and to the severity of Stratford's polarized condition. The megastructure gestures to the scale of international infrastructures and economies, while the geometry and program fulfill complex local site requirements. By inverting the Modernist "tower in the park" with a "park in the tower" typology, the Neighborhoop forces a spectacle from the uneasy tension between Stratford's role as an international hub and as a local residential neighborhood. The central courtyard, traditionally the most guarded in a residential community, is opened up to the public as a park, retail, and tourist attraction, while the geometry of the Neighborhoop affords each of the 300 apartments private garden terraces and 180-degree to 360-degree views of the London skyline.

III. STRATFORD CITY STUDIO AT YALE

ARCHITECTURAL DESIGN

AN
INCONVENIENT
TRUTH

THE PLANETARY EMERGENCY OF GLOBAL WARMING AND WHAT WE CAN DO ABOUT IT

AL GORE

→05 An Inconvenient Truth *book, 2006 (Author: Al Gore; Client: Rodale Books)*

It is evident in the world around us that very dramatic changes are taking place.

This is Mount Kilimanjaro in 1970 with its fabled snows and glaciers.

Here it is just 30 years later—with far less ice and snow.

MOUNT KILIMANJARO, TANZANIA, 1970

MOUNT KILIMANJARO, 2000.

MIKE MILLS

Since the early nineties, Mike Mills has been exploring the visual language of sixties graphics. In his early commercial work for musicians, like the Beastie Boys and Cibo Matto, and New York City boutiques, such as Supreme and X-Girl, Mills often employed pastiche to create new contexts for subcultures with their own visual codes. →01 Around 1996 Mills began making music videos for artists such as Frank Black and Air. He moved away from directing music videos to commercials and documentaries, and filmmaking became a larger part of Mills's creative output. As his filmmaking became increasingly complex, his graphics have become increasingly simple and direct. Whereas earlier work like posters for the Jon Spencer Blues Explosion (1995) were more a pastiche of fifties or sixties album art, the posters for the 2005 film *Thumbsucker* are less referential and display the traits that have come to define his graphics: simple compositions of gestural ink drawings and melancholic slogans usually set in Helvetica. →02 & →03 Mills's main graphic outlet for the past few years has been Humans, a product line that exists "between the art world and popular culture, in between graphic design and an art practice."[1] Often type based, the designs of the T-shirts, ribbons, textiles, and posters that make up the collection exhibit his trademark blend of melancholy and optimism, using Helvetica as it might be used in children's book—large and unadorned as if to indicate that the words alone are enough. And they are.

Mills has said of recent Humans pieces that he thinks of them as photography, in that they document "something that happens."[2] This statement provides insight into a piece like the cover of a record by the band The Sads. →04 Based on his Sad Poster (originally created for Humans), a text outlines a typical cycle of consumerist behavior: "I was feeling sad/I went shopping/I bought this record/I still feel sad." Mills's theory that his work is like a snapshot finds validation in this piece. A process is presented in the simplest

→01 *X-Girl T-shirt graphic, 1996 (Client: X-Girl)*

→02 *The Jon Spencer Blues Explosion poster, 1995 (Client: Matador Records)*

MIKE MILLS

manner possible—by putting words on a page in an unadorned fashion.

Mills's sensibility reflects the Modernism of the late sixties thoroughly integrated into the mainstream as the norm. Experimental Jetset have described Mills's work as "soft Modernism," a fitting description that also gets at the more romantic, human aspects of his design.

NOTES

1. *Kulturflash.net, "Artworker of the Week #51: Mike Mills," 2005.*

2. *Ibid.*

→03 *From the* Thumbsucker *promotional poster series, 2005 (Client: Mike Mills)*

I REALLY LIKED THAT THE FILM SUCKED.

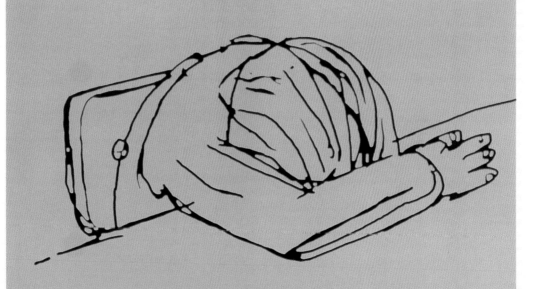

www.thumbsuckerthemovie.com
SEPTEMBER

MIKE MILLS

I Was Feeling Sad
I Went Shopping
I Bought This Record
I Still Feel Sad

→ 04 *The Sads 7" record, 2008 (Artist/Client: The Sads)*

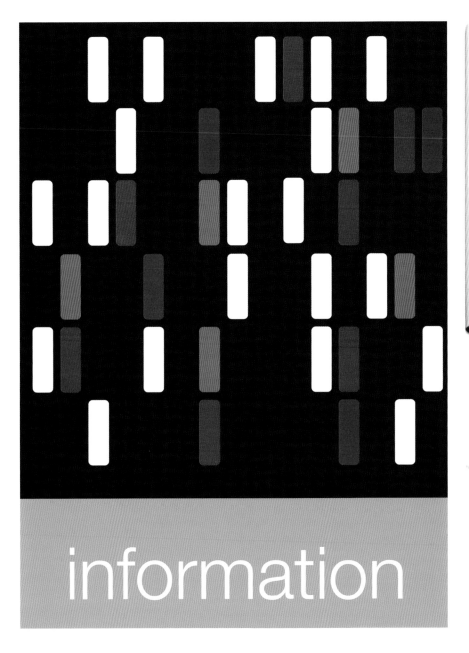

information

No one belongs here more than you. Stories by Miranda July

X·GIRL

left *From X-Girl in-store poster series, 1994–96 (Client: X-Girl)*

top right No One Belongs Here More Than You *book, 2007 (Author: Miranda July; Client: Scribner)*

bottom right *X-Girl T-shirt graphic, 1996 (Client: X-Girl)*

MIKE MILLS

"The cops are inside us." billboard, 2007
(Client: Undefeated)

Difficult Times

RUNE MORTENSEN

Norwegian designer Rune Mortensen produces iconic, restrained typographic designs for avant-garde musicians. His designs often explore a single reference point or theme and results in work that is stripped of emotional or experiential baggage. For *Live at Molde International Jazz Festival* (2002), a collaborative recording by Merzbow and Jazzkammer, Mortensen derives his solution from the setting of the recording—a jazz festival rather than from the reputations of the musicians as legends of improvised noise music. →01 The result is a subdued take on Modernism worthy of a catalog of ECM records, the German jazz label known for its subtle Modernist record covers. The cover may even mislead, as it suggests something much calmer than the maelstrom contained within.

In a design for Kevin Drumm and Lasse Marhaug's collaborative disk *Frozen by Blizzard Winds* (2002), Mortensen reflects the heavy-metal influence present in the artists' music with his choice of black-letter typeface, but stops the reference there. →02 He is careful to avoid cliches, to parody the artists' work by turning it into a pastiche of heavy-metal record covers.

A look at Mortensen's oeuvre of designs for book jackets, record sleeves, and publications reveals a consistent inventiveness and bold expressionism that goes beyond pure reductivism. His sleeves for Two Bands and a Legend's self-titled album (2007), for example, are explosions of Futura Extra Bold, echoing the free jazz this package houses, while The Brewery Tap's self-titled CD (2008) is a study in atmospheric illustration and restrained typography. →03 & →04

Throughout Mortensen's work there is a crispness and clarity, even as things get more dense and expressionistic. The bold typesetting of the words used in the watery photo-illustrations of the Anders Aarum Trio's *First Communion* CD (2006) allow the typography to retain its impact even as it ripples and distorts into abstraction. His flowing composition in the flyer for the concert series Immediate Sound at

Merzbow
Jazzkammer
Live at Molde
International
Jazz Festival

→01 Live at Molde International Jazz Festival *CD, 2001 (Artists: Merzbow and Jazzkammer; Client: Smalltown Supersound)*

→02 Frozen by Blizzard Winds *CD, 2002 (Artists: Kevin Drumm and Lasse Marhaug;*
Client: Smalltown Supersound)

RUNE MORTENSEN

The Hideout in Chicago (2007) maintains its clarity through a consistent subdivision of space. →05 It is Italian Futurism through the hands of an extremely orderly mind.

→03 Two Bands and a Legend *CD, 2007 (Artists: Cato Salsa Experience, The Thing, and Joe McPhee; Client: Smalltown Superjazz)* top *front* bottom *interior detail*

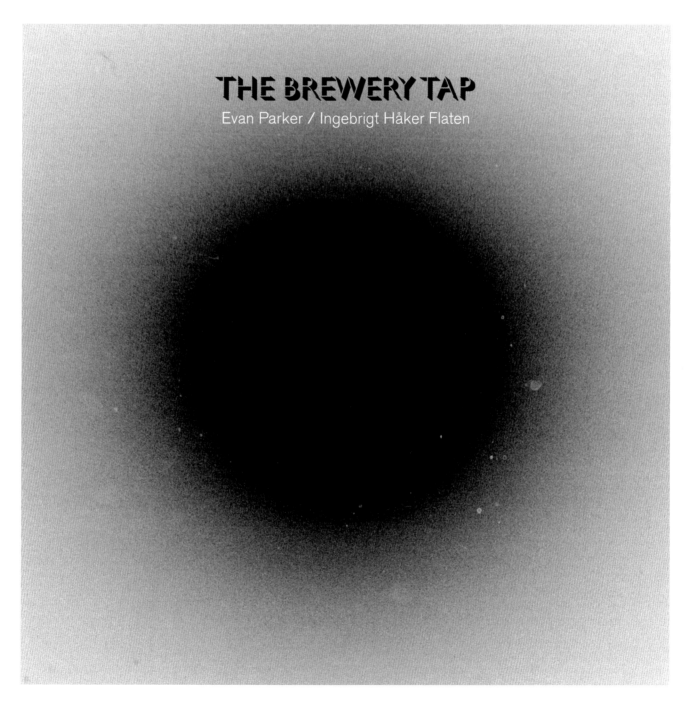

→04 The Brewery Tap *CD, 2008 (Artist: The Brewery Tap; Client: Smalltown Superjazz)*

RUNE MORTENSEN

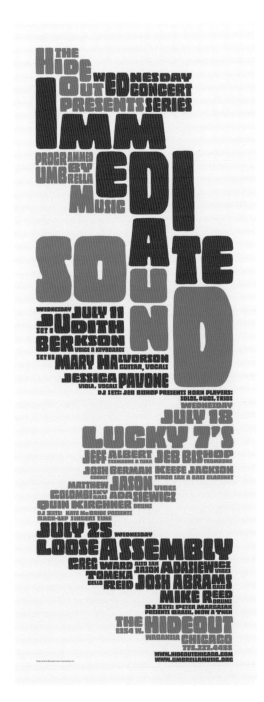

→05 *Immediate Sound flyer, 2007 (Client: The Hideout)*

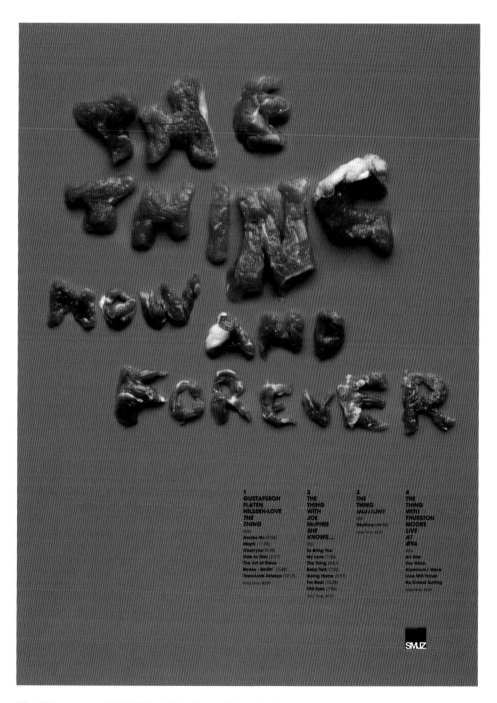

The Thing poster, 2009 (Client: Smalltown Superjazz)

ION: COBRAS

New studio album

**THE THING
ACTION JAZZ**

Mats Gustafsson
Ingebrigt Håker Flaten
Paal Nilssen-Love

«The sheer power they generate from wood, metal, breath
and muscle is stunning»
BBC

«The Thing convert nouveau
punk and vintage garage
rock into a roaring scream-
up, but the sheer energy
and love of the music keep
gimmickry at bay»
UNCUT

SMJZ

www.smalltownsuperjazz.com
STSJ123CD

A MOMENT

NOT A SOMBRE RE

IT IS NOICE CRYING

THE THING
A TRAUMA

THE
THING
ACTION
JAZZ

above and opposite top row Action Jazz *CD, 2006 (Artist: The Thing; Client: Smalltown Superjazz)*

Shinjuku Crawl *CD, 2009 (Artist: The Thing with Otomo Yoshihide; Client: Smalltown Superjazz)*

RUNE MORTENSEN

Splatter *CD, 2007 (Artists: Paul Nilssen-Love and Mats Gustaffson; Client: Smalltown Superjazz)*

Live at Cosmopolite DVD, 2010 (Artist: Jaga Jazzist; Client: Smalltown Supersound)

NEUE

Mark Blamire has been championing the work of the new Modernism through his online shop and exhibition space, Blanka, for more than eight years. Whether it be selling the printed work of Spin and Design Project, commissioning prints and T-shirts from Build, or reprinting classic Wim Crouwel posters, Blamire has worked tirelessly to promote those designers who are continuing the legacy of European Modernism and shedding light on its roots.

It is no surprise that Blamire's own work as Neue from 2000 to 2005 tends toward the same aesthetic as the peers he promotes. Working largely for the music industry in the earlier part of this decade designing covers for a variety of dance artists and labels (including Simple, which he cofounded in 2003), he helped to define the look of electronic music. The graphic language of Neue is a kind of technical Modernism—featuring geometric graphics or lush photography and a single weight of Helvetica Neue on a visible grid. Blamire's record covers are interesting for the way that the typography is a supporting player to the iconic images and yet so integral to the overall aesthetic—it is difficult to imagine these covers without the marriage of image and type. The fact that these designs look so effortless speaks volumes about Blamire's skill.

In 2005 Blamire left commission-based design to focus all his energies on Blanka. His passion for Modernism and graphic design has resulted in projects like 50 (Design Museum, London, 2007), an exhibition, with which he celebrated the fiftieth anniversary of Helvetica by commissioning fifty posters (one for each year) by fifty different designers. (See pages 24–29 for an interview with Blamire.)

Hum flyer, 2005 (Client: Hum)

From: blam@blanka.co.uk
Subject: 50
Date: 1 March 2007 23:44:42 GMT
To: candyculture@gmail.com

The Bridge on the River Kwai [1957] Vertigo [1958]
North by Northwest [1959] Ben-Hur [1960]
The Guns of Navarone [1961] Spartacus [1962]
The Great Escape [1963] Zulu [1964] Goldfinger [1965]
The Good, the Bad and the Ugly [1966]
Cool Hand Luke [1967] Planet of the Apes [1968]
The Italian Job [1969] Tora! Tora! Tora! [1970]
The French Connection [1971] The Godfather [1972]
The Sting [1973] The Godfather II [1974] Jaws [1975]
All the President's Men [1976] Star Wars [1977]
Close Encounters of the Third Kind [1978] Alien [1979]
Raging Bull [1980] Raiders of the Lost Ark [1981]
Blade Runner [1982] Scarface [1983] The Terminator [1984]
Ran [1985] Aliens [1986] The Untouchables [1987]
Dangerous Liaisons [1988] My Left Foot [1989]
Goodfellas [1990] Boyz N the Hood [1991] Reservoir Dogs [1992]
Schindler's List [1993] Leon [1994] Heat [1995] Romeo & Juliet [1996]
Life is Beautiful [1997] Run Lola Run [1998]
The Sixth Sense [1999] O Brother, Where Art Thou? [2000]
The Fellowship of the Ring [2001] The Pianist [2002]
Kill Bill [2003] Eternal Sunshine of the Spotless Mind [2004]
Sin City [2005] Apocalypto [2006] Helvetica [2007]

Films chosen are taken from those on general release at cinemas [1957-2007] Data taken from Wikipedia

50 poster, 2007 (Client: self-published)

Trainspotting *poster, 1996 (Client: FFI)*

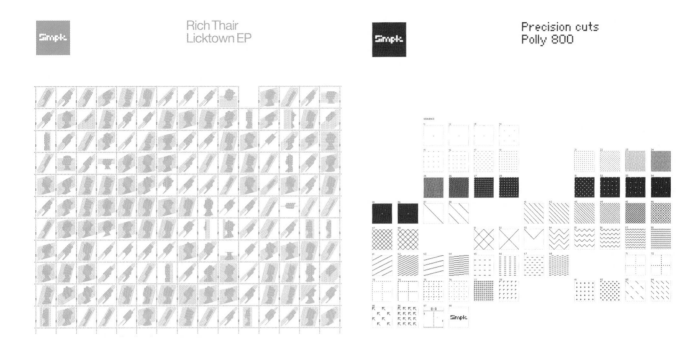

Simpk.

Rich Thair
Licktown EP

Simpk.

Precision cuts
Polly 800

Licktown EP *12" record, 2005 (Artist: Rich Thair;*
Client: Simple Records)

Polly 800 *12" record, 2005 (Artist: Precision Cuts;*
Client: Simple Records)

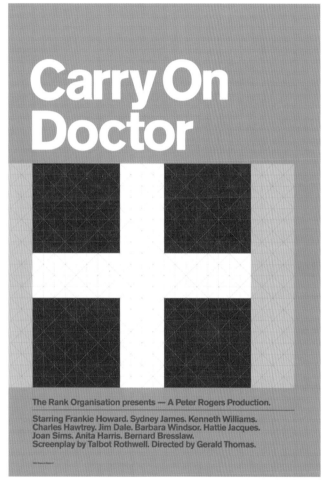

Carry On poster series, 2008 (Client: self-published)

Solid-body electric 1946-1965

The pre-CBS Stratocaster [Tremolo arm not shown]
Designed by Leo Fender, Freddie Tavares, George Fullerton

American archtops

"Violin-makers have certainly been an inspiration to me - more so than guitar makers really... A violin is either right of it's wrong - theres very little room for subjectivity, and violin players are more in agreement than guitarists on what their instruments should play and feel and sound like."
Robert Benedetto

top row *Space Between CD, 2005 (Artist: Will Saul; Client: Simple Records)*

bottom left *Fender Stratocaster 1954/ Benedetto Manhattan 16" poster (Client: self-published)*

bottom right *Fox Linton invitation (Client: Fox Linton)*

Roger
Sanchez

Another
Chance

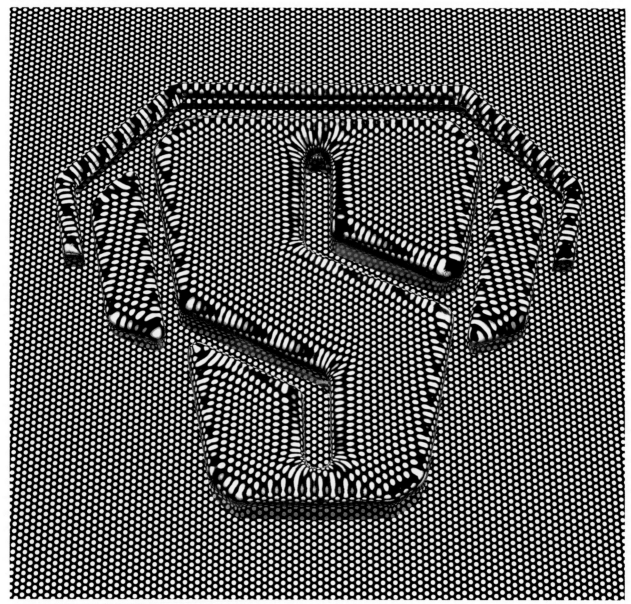

Another Chance *12" record, 2001 (Artist: Roger Sanchez; Client: Dance Pool)*

Royal Flush *12" record, 2004 (Artist: Precision Cuts; Client: Simple Records)*

PROJECT PROJECTS

Project Projects works largely with cultural institutions, producing designs for museums, galleries, and nonprofits. The firm represents a shift in American design and typography—from the clever pastiche-oriented design often celebrated in design annuals to one where type usage is functional. The type choices they make are open-ended, which helps create a tone rather than a definitive concept. The firm first often establishes the context by looking at the environment a piece functions in and works its way inward from there.

In their design program for the public art exhibition/initiative The Good Life (Pier 40, New York City, 2006), they appear to have worked from the macro to the micro, starting with a simple type treatment on an oversized yellow balloon and then interpreting the balloon as a simple logo. →01 Each iteration of the design program builds in visual complexity by adding pattern to an ever-present grid. Project Projects never attempt to complicate the typography itself or make the type do much more than articulate the words that need to be communicated.

A bold Brutalist style is at play in their recent publications like the architectural zine *Sur Las Pavés La Ferme!* (Over the pavement, the farm!, 2008) and *Stan VanDerBeek* (2007), a retrospective catalog for the artist of the same name. →02 & →03 The typography of *Stan VanDerBeek* explodes off the cover. The impact is heightened by the use of half-sheet (a sheet of paper bound to the spine of the book that covers a vertical half of the front and back covers) on which the introductory text is placed. The juxtaposition of the smaller-size essay text with the bold all-over type of the title sets up the extreme contrasts that follow. Huge underlined type is used on all the section dividers, where it plows over the background photos of artworks. The same bold typeface is used for the running heads and page numbers, which adds a dark black mark to every page and runs over photography and artworks. The section containing an interview

→01 *The Good Life exhibition, 2006 (Client: Van Alen Institute)* top *exhibition collateral* bottom *exterior view of exhibition space*

The Good Life exhibition, 2006 (Client: Van Alen Institute)

is set in a thinner typewriter font that creates an overall light-gray field and makes for a severe contrast between the running headers and the interview text. The experience of reading *Stan VanDerBeek* is a back-and-forth between high-contrast relationships within the various visual elements and the Brutalist section dividers where black type is laid over black-and-white images in a way that creates subtle color relationships that make bold statements. As was the case in the firm's work for The Good Life, the typeface choices are not dictated by a clear or obvious concept. The grotesque sans-serif typeface used throughout echoes American Modernist design of the sixties and seventies but is not an overt pastiche of those time periods.

Their design of an identity system for the Rachel Uffner Gallery (New York City, 2008) displays the same suggestive quality. →04 It is based around a customized version of the seventies typeface Trooper Roman. The design doesn't scream "1975." Instead, it is a subtle reference to the exuberant, more eclectic Modernism practiced in the United States at the time by designers like Herb Lubalin. The simple Brutalist compositions and use of overprinted metallics give it a contemporary feel that sets it apart from pure nostalgia.

→02 Sur Las Pavés La Ferme! *(Over the pavement, the farm!) book, 2008 (Author: Project Projects and WORKac; Client: WORKac)*

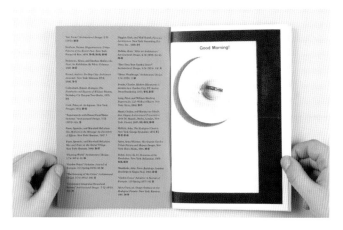

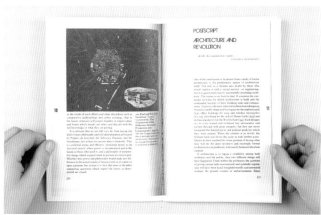

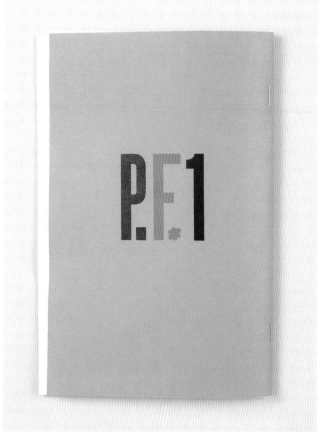

PROJECT PROJECTS

→03 Stan VanDerBeek *book, 2007 (Author/Client: Guild & Greyshkul)*

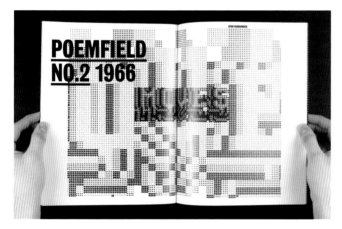

PROJECT PROJECTS

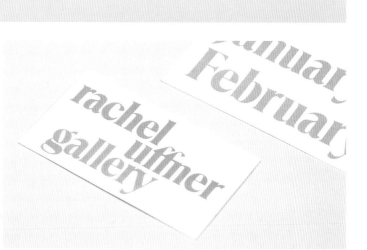

→04 *Rachel Uffner Gallery identity system, 2008*
(Client: Rachel Uffner Gallery)

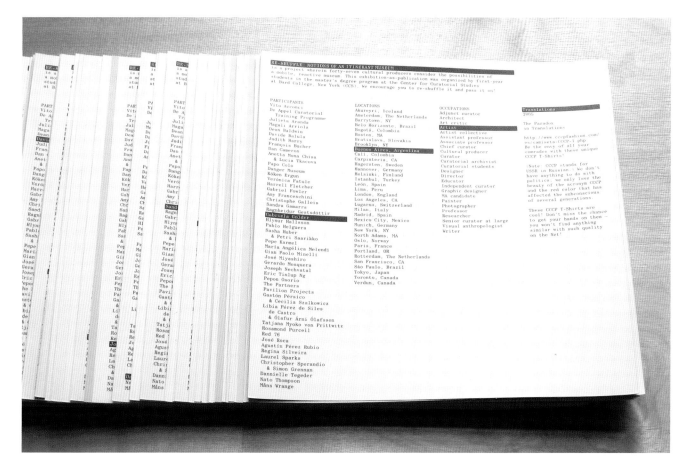

Re-Shuffle/Notions of an Itinerant Museum *exhibition catalog, 2006*
(Author/Client: Bard College Center for Curatorial Studies)

PROJECT PROJECTS

3 Dinners
37 Participants
1 Book

Who Cares brings together inspiring artists, curators, and scholars to consider the urgent issues of art's relationship to social action today.

ISBN-10: 1-928570-02-X
ISBN-13: 978-1-928570-02-8
51500

9 781928 570028

US $15.00

Who Cares

WHO CARES

CREATIVETIMEBOOKS

Doug Ashford
Julie Ault
Gregg Bordowitz
Tania Bruguera
Paul Chan
Mel Chin
Dean Daderko
Peter Eleey
Coco Fusco
Chitra Ganesh
Deborah Grant
Hans Haacke
K8 Hardy
Sharon Hayes
Emily Jacir
Ronak Kapadia
Byron Kim
Steve Kurtz
Julian LaVerdiere
Lucy Lippard
Marlene McCarty
John Menick
Helen Molesworth
Anne Pasternak
Heather Peterson
Paul Pfeiffer
Patricia C. Phillips
Michael Rakowitz
Ben Rodriguez-Cubeñas
Martha Rosler
Ralph Rugoff
Amy Sillman
Allison Smith
Kiki Smith
David Levi Strauss
Nato Thompson
The Yes Men

Who Cares *book, 2006 (Author/Client: Creative Time Books)*

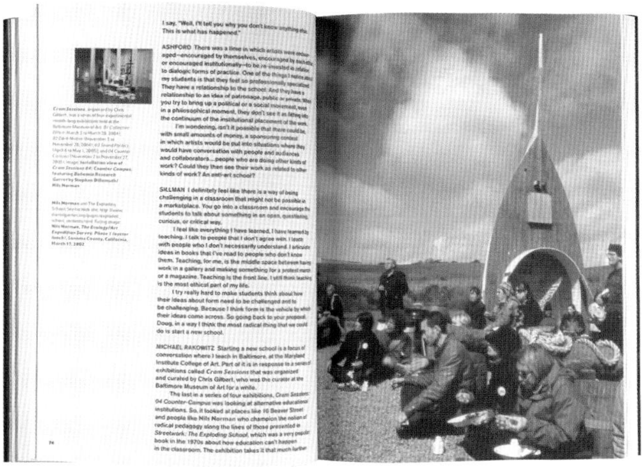

I say, "Well, I'll tell you why you don't know anything else. This is what has happened."

ASHFORD There was a time in which artists were encouraged—encouraged by themselves, encouraged by institutions, or encouraged institutionally—to be re-invested in relation to dialogic forms of practice. One of the things I notice about my students is that they feel so professionally specialized. They have a relationship to the school. And they have a relationship to an idea of patronage, public or private. Now you try to bring up a political or a social movement, not in a philosophical moment, they don't see it as being the continuum of the institutional placement of the work.

I'm wondering, isn't it possible that there could be, with small amounts of money, a sponsoring school in which artists would be put into situations where they would have conversation with people and audiences and collaborators... people who are doing other kinds of work? Could they then see their work as related to other kinds of work? An anti-art school?

SILLMAN I definitely feel like there is a way of being challenging in a classroom that might not be positive in a marketplace. You go into a classroom and encourage the students to talk about something in an open, questioning, curious, or critical way.

I feel like everything I have learned, I have learned by teaching. I talk to people that I don't agree with. I work with people who I don't necessarily understand. I answer ideas in books that I've read to people who don't have them. Teaching, for me, is the middle space between hard work in a gallery and making something for a printed matter or a magazine. Teaching is the front line. I still think teaching is the most ethical part of my life.

I try really hard to make students think about how their ideas about home need to be challenged and to be challenging. Because I think home in the vehicle by which their ideas come across. So going back to your proposal, Doug, in a way I think the most radical thing that we can do is start a new school.

MICHAEL RAKOWITZ Starting a new school is a kind of conversation where I teach in Baltimore, at the Maryland Institute College of Art. Part of it is in response to a series of exhibitions called Crane Sessions that was organized and curated by Chris Gilbert, who was the curator at the Baltimore Museum of Art for a while.

The last in a series of four exhibitions, Crane Session: 04 Counter-Campus was looking at alternative educational institutions. So, it looked at places like 16 Beaver Street and people like Nils Norman who champion the value of radical pedagogy along the lines of those presented in Sametwork: The Exploding School, which was a very popular book in the 1970s about how education can't happen in the classroom. The exhibition takes it that much further

From Session: *In and In* by Chris Gilbert, and a series of four experimental month-long organizations held at the Baltimore Museum of Art. B Collection 2004 Crane Counter-Campus. 04 Counter-Campus September 3 to November 14, 2004, and Grand Rapids April 6 to May 1, 2005, and Crane Session: Countersite 04 November 3 to November 27, 2004—image Installation view of Crane Session: 04: Counter-Campus featuring Between Research Abstract by Stephen Willdraw/ Nils Norman.

Nils Norman and The Exploding School Some books are my algo from co-organizer eco-logos related to urban, architecture living design Nils Norman, The Exploding Expedition Survey, Phase I (summer field), Cascadia County, California, March 17, 2001

---

organized *In Mourning and In Rage*, a response to the sensational media coverage surrounding the Los Angeles Hillside Strangler. She used the media as a performance venue by designing a press event as a performance. (For a full description of the project see Moira Roth, "Interview with Suzanne Lacy," 1990, http://www.aaa.si.edu/ collections/oralhistories/transcripts/ lacy90.htm (accessed June 10, 2006).)

Mel Chin, Truth Hertz, June 20,1994

ARTISTS CALL Against U.S. Intervention in Central America was a nationwide mobilization of writers, artists, activists, artist organizations, and solidarity groups that began in New York in 1983. Quickly mobilizing artists and their organizations across the country, ARTISTS CALL collectively produced over two hundred exhibitions, concerts, and other public events over a period of twelve months. These events increased awareness of our government's involvement in state terrorism across the hemisphere, linked the notion of aesthetic emancipation to revolutionary politics, and provided concrete resources for the cultural workers, and public intellectuals in the region and in exile. An excerpt from the ARTISTS CALL general statement published in January 1984 reads, "If, as artists, we can silently witness the destruction of other cultures, we forfeit the right to make art of our own." Image: Peter Gourfain, Button for ARTISTS CALL Against U.S. Intervention in Central America, 1984

to have been lost, or wasn't picked up by other artists.

CHIN But now the media is multinational; they are global networks. The Yes Men have been able to do some amazing incursions into it. My own incursions were not so much planned artworks, but ways to find out what motivates media so I did some experiments. I was selling O. J. Simpson T-shirts in front of the Los Angeles Courthouse on the day of his arraignment. The shirts said, "Truth Hertz"—neither guilty nor innocent, justice was for lease.

It was a weird experience. Because, at the same time, there was an activist demonstration in the street against violence against women, with actresses. And everybody had their O.J. T-shirts. Suddenly the cameras noticed and someone said, just like wildfire, "They're merchandising murder." And the cameras flipped and they spent all their time on the vendors. The whole day was spent on that.

So the question becomes: How do you even create the methodology to spark another kind of attitude? How do you use rumor effectively?

The point of sharing this story was that I was surprised I was doing this research, but trying not to be an artist. Instead, I was trying to make a couple bucks and cash in like those vendors in the street. And then I learned something about how the street reacts. It's almost like we have to hit the streets again in order to see what they are about.

ASHFORD Over the years there have been so many projects that have created a symbolic power from human interaction and today such protest is either not growing into larger forms of public expression or isn't being supported by art institutions.

As artists, we've banded together periodically. A great example is something Lucy Lippard, Martha Rosler, and I were involved in, ARTISTS CALL Against U.S. Intervention in Central America in 1984. It mobilized art institutions across the whole country—from galleries to museums to the covers of magazines—to speak out publicly against U.S. military intervention in this hemisphere.

LIPPARD Thirty cities across the country, some thirty galleries in New York City, and some events in Canada too.

came out for the Republican National Convention, how were they gotten out? I'm a dinosaur since I'm not even on the Internet and don't do e-mail. I live off the grid, I haul water, and so forth; I'm like in another world. So, I'm curious, what type of community access do we have now? Was the organizing all done on the Internet? No more getting small groups together and getting them to go out and have more meetings...none of that?

PASTERNAK There doesn't seem to be much of that kind of intimate organizing. There has been a recent shift in public opinion about the war in Iraq. Do you think it is related to activism or that it's the result of the media's change in strategy?

LIPPARD Well, the media has to pick up on some things that are going on, but they control the spin.

ROSLER Yeah. I heard some guy on the radio this morning, a political correspondent for The Daily News, the chief of their Washington bureau. He said forty-seven times, "The American public has made up its mind about Iraq. It knows what it thinks."

BONANNO (THE YES MEN) Mm-hmm. But I think that what Lucy just said is kind of critical. Right now, we could organize a flash mob over the Internet that could maybe get a couple of thousand people to show up at an instant to do something ridiculous in any given place. The Internet creates a context for social networks, but it doesn't actually make them. And I think that's why our friend, "Bob," who I referred to earlier, says that art isn't activism. I think this is the critical issue, what kind of networks are those and are they temporary or are they more sustaining?

ASHFORD We know that those social networks are there, we also know that there are coherent communities that exist and we know that there's a sense of public outrage. Why is it so difficult for artists to be put into sustainable working relationships with those communities?

We seek people out individually in our practices. We're asked by curators and organizers to do a project at this festival location or this biennial and we participate in it, site-specifically as artists parachuted in as social actors. It's often a short-term relationship. But there are many other

Anywhere in the World
Collaboration 1
November 14, 2005

The Yes Men discussion was motivated by the cultural phenomenon of the Yes Men and urban art festivals, and their paradoxical affinity with the growth of transnational corporate power. A number of globalized industrial and economic practices—notably the outsourcing and distribution of individuals and labor, often without ties to any particular city, country, or continent—have resonance with the way artists today are asked to be both everywhere and nowhere, and their practices transportable, transferable, yet in some way specific to their location or community of presentation. In this context, a curatorial practice is challenged to map and model new symptoms of economy and occupancy.

But in the post-9/11 moment, the promise of participatory and open art has been emptied art practices has been met by formidable barriers to free economic assistance and expression. When one considers this in light of the history of the institutionalized "community-based" practices of the 1990s, and the political functions that inhibit those seeking to freely fund, in an almost mythical nature of practice begin to take shape. It is worth noting, then, that this discussion begins with a kind of project of ideas because the nature of artistic expression through the participatory and social experiences, from the lightening of security in the reaction of a fearful public.

The dialogue touches upon the need for discussion about places, what a people can come together and share discussions on art and sound power and architecture into those spaces have enriched urban centers in the past. Many participants communicated their belief that local issues become sustained nourishment by a broader audience and how large. The mouth of the conversation, the participants consider ways in which art practices can create dialogic and collective representations and allies. Although the discussion evokes the question of art's political efficacy, eventually the group focuses on how to use topical the ideologically productive tensions between art and the intersection of socially sustained forms. It is a matter of core of new audiences, their politics, and the practices that might sustain them.

Project Row Houses is a neighborhood-based art and cultural organization located in Houston, Texas's Third Ward. It was established in 1993 on a site of twenty-two abandoned shotgun houses to connect the work of artists with the revitalization of the community. The project was inspired by the work of African-American artist Dr. John Biggers, who celebrated the social significance of the shotgun house community in his paintings.

Part of a project, organized by four video artists including Íñigo Manglano-Ovalle. The project taught video techniques to over fifty teenagers from Chicago's West Town neighborhood, who represented their lives and experiences on the twenty-five monitors installed up and down the street. The success of the event led to the founding of Street-Level Youth Media, a storefront project that teaches kids media literacy and video production skills.

MANUEL RAEDER

Navigating Manuel Raeder's website is not unlike experiencing his books, installations, and self-published works. The website is raw, seemingly simple, but at times bewildering. There is a thumbnail for every project, displayed at what appears to be random sizes and butted up one next to another to offer a disorienting sea of choices. Clicking on the thumbnail for one of his book projects might lead to anything from a view of fourteen-pages of spreads that show how a book unfolds to a small photo of the cover and a publisher's link. Like Raeder's approach to design, each item is governed by its own logic.

Throughout his work there is a push against standardization, toward unexpected uses of formats. Says Raeder, "I'm concerned with how you can change modes of production, be it editing a text differently, printing a book in another way, or using a book binder's machine in a way that will make the structure of the book more visible."[1]

With each project, he analyzes the subject matter and the context to find a unique starting point. His design for *The Inner Voice* (2005), a monograph on German performance artist and ventriloquist Asta Gröting, employs a custom-made typeface, Inner Voice, that references vintage theater fonts. →01 This typeface is used for all the headlines in the book in an open-ended manner—it maintains a direct relationship to the size of the image. The text portions of the book are designed with a very simple two-column grid that allows for the constant size shifts in the headlines and images, giving the book a rhythm while still maintaining some consistency.

In other projects, such as with the second issue of his self-published magazine *What is this? What is that? Who are they? and where do they come from?* (in collaboration with Ella Klaschka), Raeder questions what a magazine is. →02 This simple no-budget publication captures much of what is intriguing about Raeder's work. A tentative, abstract form adorns the cover of a booklet of which the first page contains the

INNER VOICE
FONT ABCDEF
GHIJKLMNOP
QRSTUVWXY
Z abcdefghijk
lmnopqrstuv
wxyz!?",,@%
»,.–ı^•&/()12
34567890

→01 *Inner Voice typeface, 2005*
(Client: self-published)

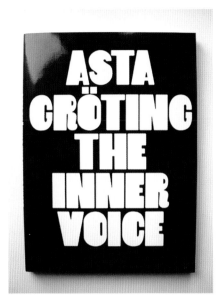

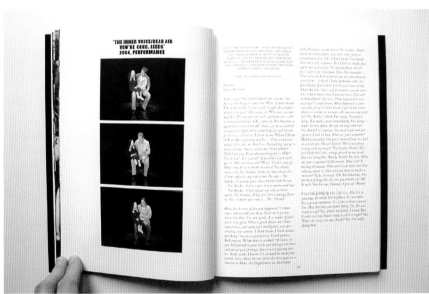

→01 The Inner Voice *book, 2005 (Author: Asta Gröting;*
Client: Revolver Verlag)

MANUEL RAEDER

title in simple hand-drawn type. Every subsequent page is blank, including the oversized tan centerfold (a submission by artist Ed Fella), which extends past the edges of the book block. The second-to-last page reads, "No topics, dominant ideas or central themes. Capable of spontaneous movements." By calling what is essentially a sketchbook or notepad a magazine, Raeder and Klaschka fundamentally change our relationship with it. In much of Raeder's work and collaborations, simple gestures build upon each other to create strange, thoughtful, and beautiful objects.

NOTES

1. Manuel Raeder, interview with the author, 2009.

Happening & Fluxus: Kölnischer Kunstverein, 1970 exhibition announcement, 2007 (Client: Kölnischer Kunstverein)

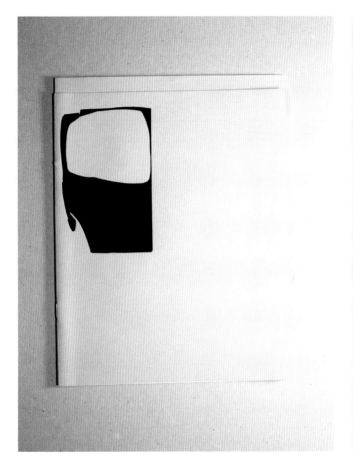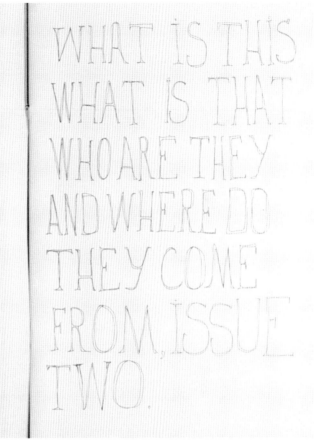

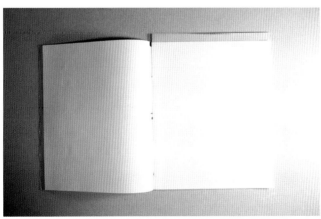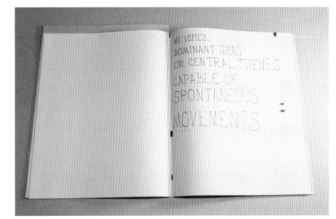

→02 What is this? What is that? Who are they? and where do they come from? *magazine, 2003 (Collaboration with Ella Klaschka; Client: self-published)*

Godville

Omer Fast

ABCDEFGHIJK

LMNOPQRSTU

VWXYZabcdfeg

hijklmnopqrstuv

wxyz1234567890

!"§$&/()=?`'_:;

Godville typeface, 2005 (Client: self-published)

Art Berlin Contemporary exhibition signage, 2008 (Client: Art Berlin Contemporary)

MANUEL RAEDER

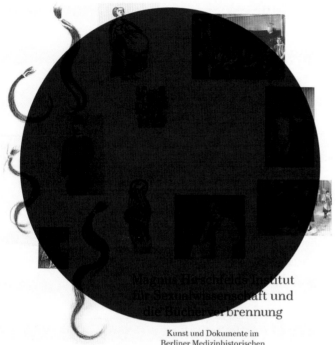

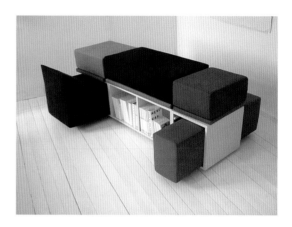

left *Sex Brennt (Sex burns) poster, 2008 (Client: Berlin Medical Historical Museum of the Charité)*

top right *Which One Chair furniture system (Client: self-published)*

bottom right *Composite Greetings furniture system for displaying postcards (Client: self-published)*

SIB-

LINGS

AND

TWINS

SIBLINGS AND TWINS

HAEGUE
YANG

Portikus
Alte Brücke 2/Maininsel
D-60594 Frankfurt am Main
www.portikus.de

Eröffnung: 16.5.08 ab 20 Uhr
17.5.-29.6.08

Dienstag-Sonntag, 11-18 Uhr
Mittwoch, 11-20 Uhr
Montag geschlossen

Siblings and Twins exhibition announcement, 2008 (Client: Portikus)

MANUEL RAEDER

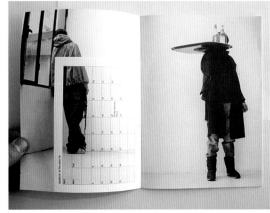

Bless *lookbook, 2005 (Client: Bless)*

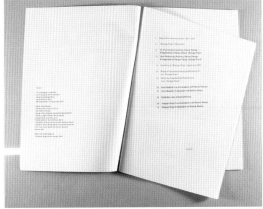

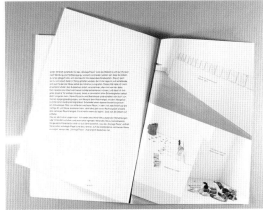

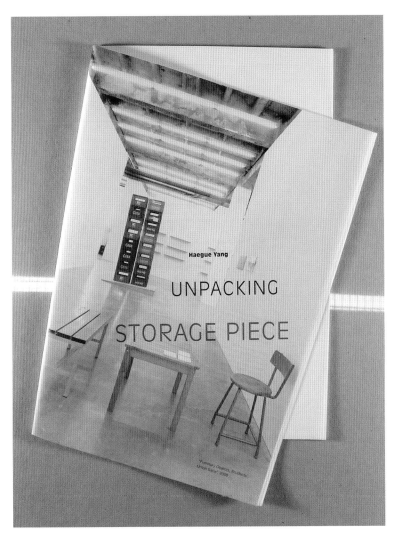

Unpacking Storage Piece *exhibition catalog, 2007*
(Author: Haegue Yang; Client: Wiens Verlag)

RESEARCH AND DEVELOPMENT

In 2001 British designer and educator John Morgan wrote "The Vow of Chastity," a set of rules inspired by Dogme 95's "Vow of Chastity" that forbade special effects, background music, or the use of dollies and special lighting in film.[1] Morgan's vow was given to his first-year graphic design students at Central St. Martin's College of Art (London), with the intent countering "certain [unnamed] tendencies in graphic design at St. Martins." The rules included: "Content Matters: Design nothing that is not worth reading," "The book must be hand-held (and designed from the inside out)," "Photoshop/Illustrator filters are forbidden," "The design must not contain any superficial elements," and "Genre design is not acceptable (…No superficial application of style)."[2] While Morgan's manifesto was a tongue-in-cheek response to the overuse of style or "the superficial application" of it by students, the Swedish design studio Research and Development may have unknowingly answered Morgan's call for a more organic, content-driven design.

Research and Development's work is defined by an informal approach to the use of the grid. Their book design for *Design: Stockholm* (2005) presents photographs seemingly tossed arbitrarily across the spreads and locked onto an underlying structure. →01 The results are dynamic yet ordered. What separates this from a more Modernist approach is that while the photo arrangements are orderly, they are hardly systemic. Research and Development uses the grid as a puzzle to be completed.

Research and Development's first works, like their campaign identity for the Stockholm School of Entrepreneurship (2004), favored a more Helvetica-heavy approach. →02 While these pieces are striking, as they recall the more rigid Modernism of Swiss Typography, their work has increasingly taken on a more organic, seemingly more direct, undesigned feel. The grids and use of size contrasts in their early work seem premeditated—as if the designs

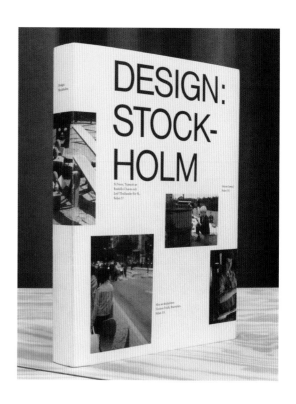

→01 Design: Stockholm *book, 2005*
(Author/Client: Design Stockholm)

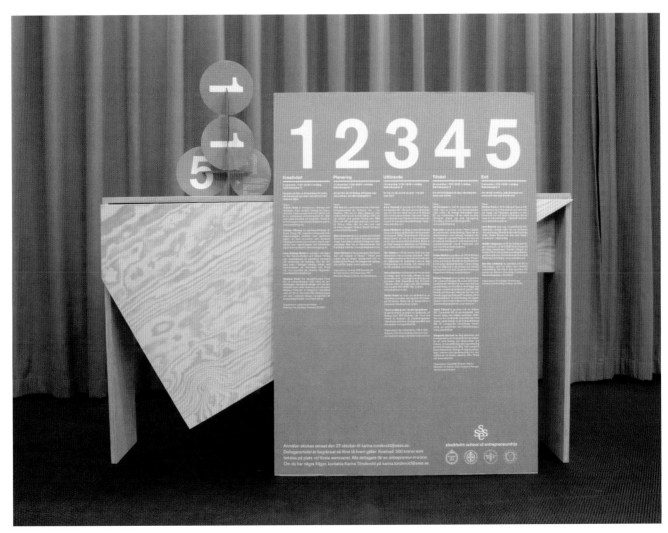

→02 top *Stockholm School of
Entrepreneurship poster and
promotion, 2004 (Client: Stockholm
School of Entrepreneurship)*

→03 *Vårsalongen Formbart exhibition, 2005 (Client: Vårsalongen Formbart)*
bottom left *catalog* bottom right *exterior signage*

RESEARCH AND DEVELOPMENT

were planned first and then content forced into them. Contrast that approach with the Design: Stockholm identity (2005). The type is still Helvetica, buts its usage is Brutalist and feels like it could be a default-font option rather than an premeditated style.

The informal approach is even more evident in their work for Vårsalongen Formbart (Stockholm, 2005), an exhibition of design, fashion, and crafts. →03 The promotional posters document exhibition pieces as they were being unpacked. Bubble-wrap still protects them, and a simple serif-type treatment frames the photography. In the exhibition catalog, Research and Development document the process of shooting all the work, leaving the backdrop visible. The catalog begins and ends with photos of the copy stand used to document the pieces.

As Research and Development's work evolves, each piece of their body of work becomes less a singular statement than an open-ended question about content and its form.

NOTES

1. In 1995 Danish filmmakers Lars von Trier and Thomas Vinterberg started Dogme 95, a movement that intended to introduce a new realism and purity into filmmaking.

2. Michael Bierut, William Drenttel, and Stephen Heller, eds., Looking Closer 4: Critical Writings on Graphic Design (New York City: Allworth Press, 2002), 114.

Cap&Design *magazine, 2007 (Client: Cap&Design)*

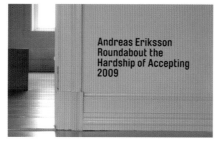

Momentum: 5th Nordic Biennial of Contemporary Art identity system, 2009
(Client: Nordic Biennial of Contemporary Art)

RESEARCH AND DEVELOPMENT

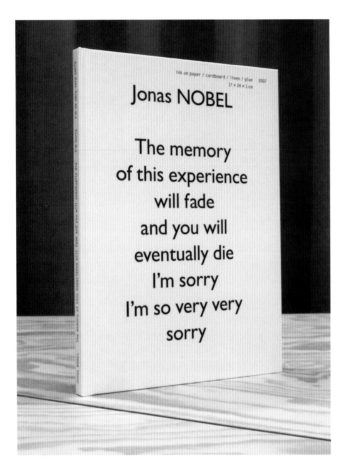

The memory of this experience will fade and you will eventually die, I'm sorry, I'm so very very sorry book, *2007 (Author: Jonas Nobel; Client: Galleri Charlotte Lund)*

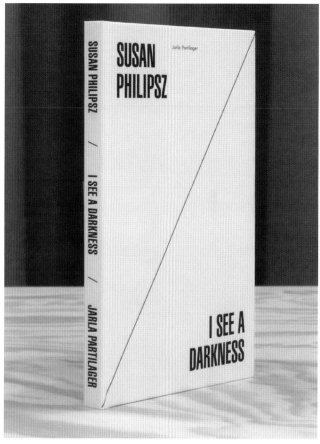

Lunds konsthall exhibition catalogs, 2008–9
(Client: Lunds konsthall)

I See a Darkness *artist's book, 2009*
(Author: Susan Philipsz; Client: Jarla Partilager)

RESEARCH AND DEVELOPMENT

Olafur Eliasson: Winter Solstice exhibition invitation, 2007 (Client: Jarla Partilager)

An Alternative Guide to Palais de Tokyo *guidebook, 2006 (Author: Research and Development; Client: Palais de Tokyo)*

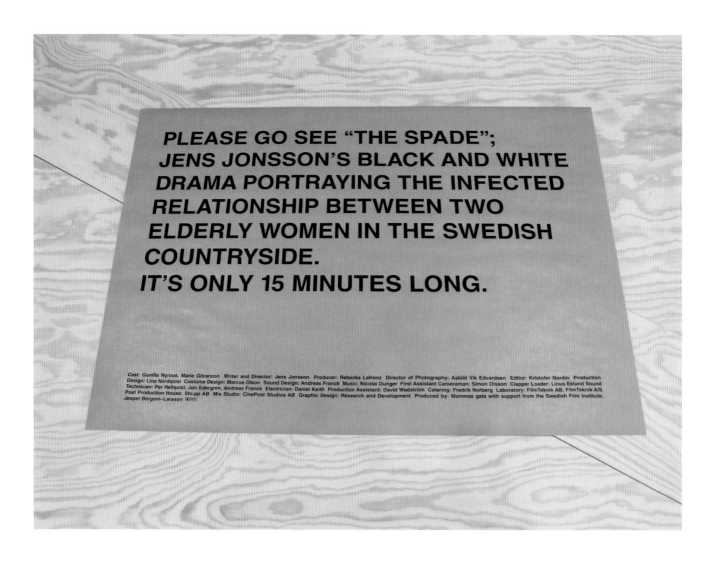

The Spade flyer, 2003 (Client: Jens Jonsson)

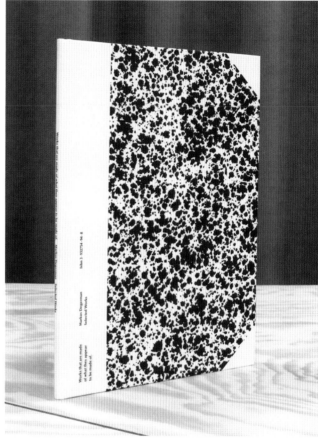

A Better Life through Design *promotional brochure, 2009*
(Client: The Swedish Society of Crafts and Design)

Works that are made of what they appear to be
made of *book, 2008 (Author: Markus Degerman;*
Client: Kunstlerhaus Bethaniend)

MATTHEW REZAC

The work of Matthew Rezac is marked by a utilitarian typography that is supported by a visually rich approach to printing and photographic art direction. His publication designs, in particular, take advantage of print effects, such as die cuts and overprinting of inks, to build upon a core concept. The exhibition catalog (designed in collaboration with Andrew Blauvelt) for the 2008 01SJ Biennial: Superlight (01SJ Biennial, San Jose, 2008) avoids the use of cliches like LED typefaces and digital textures that are associated with digital art and instead concerns itself with the idea of light. →01 The main typeface is a soft, chunky serif with a more general appeal than would be expected from purely digital art. Process colors overprinting on black, tinted varnishes, and translucent sheets are all used to examine this exploration of light. Additionally, the visible spectrum of light is used throughout the book as an organizing principle by assigning specific content to different color fields.

Rezac spent two years as a design fellow at the Walker Art Center in Minneapolis, an institution whose design is best known for the use of simple but distinctive typography and materials—unusual book bindings, shifting paper stocks—that relates to the content. This influence can be seen in Rezac's work. The catalog *WARM: A Feminist Art Collective in Minnesota* (2006) by Joanna Inglot, for the exhibition of the same name, is a history of the group. →02 WARM originally began as a slide registry of female artists in Minnesota. Rezac selects a representative slide of each of the twelve artists to reproduce on the inside of the oversized dust jacket, which is folded in an unconventional manner to reveal the slide images between the folds. The book is made up of three sections—a historical text, additional essays, and the plates—each color-coded in a way that is visible in the exposed binding. The typography tends toward a mix of soft serif and finely detailed text typefaces, none of which screams too loudly as to its exact

→01 Superlight *book, 2008 (Designed with Andrew Blauvelt; Author/Client: ZERO1)*

Published on the occasion of the 2008 01SJ
Biennial: A Global Festival of Art on the Edge and
the exhibition Superlight, which were organized
and curated by Steve Dietz for ZER01.

The 2008 01SJ Biennial was held June 4–8, 2008,
in San Jose, California. The 2006 01SJ Biennial,
held in conjunction with the 13th International
Symposium on Electronic Art ISEA 2006, took
place August 7–13, 2006.

The exhibition Superlight was coproduced
by the San Jose Museum of Art.

San Jose Museum of Art, San Jose, CA
May 10–August 31, 2008

Cleveland Museum of Contemporary Art,
Cleveland, OH
January 23–May 10, 2009

This publication is made possible by support from
the Andy Warhol Foundation for the Visual Arts.

Sponsors of ZER01 and the 01SJ Biennial are listed
in this volume on pages 238 and 420.

First Edition © 2009 ZER01

A Cataloging-in-Publication record for this book
is available from the Library of Congress.

ISBN 978 0 982145 80 7

Designers
Andrew Blauvelt and Matthew Rezac

Editor
Pamela Johnson

Curatorial Publications Intern
Margaretha Haughwout

Color Separations
Shapco Printing, Inc.

Printed and bound in the United States
by Shapco Printing, Inc.

Superlight
and the 2008
01SJ Biennial:
A Global
Festival of Art
on the Edge are
presented by
ZER01.

**Fashionably Late for
the Relationship**
2008
Interactive three channel video installation

MATTHEW REZAC

intentions. It is this use of typefaces that helps to keep Rezac's work free of genre associations—it is not a simple equation of this typeface = this idea. Instead, it is a mix of typefaces, with each assigned to a different role, that organizes the book's hierarchy.

In a number of works for the Minneapolis College of Art & Design (MCAD), Rezac explored letters as physical objects. →03 & 04 *Become*, the MCAD 2007 viewbook, transformed the studios, classrooms, and galleries of the school into temporary typographic installations with letters printed out on paper and forming words hung up on their walls. These were then photographed; the resulting images were used in spreads that marked the catalog's different sections. The realism of the photography often contrasted with flat illustrations, referencing the mark-making inherent in painting and drawings. These illustrations also acted as frames for more detailed typography.

In his work Rezac connects content to form in tangible ways, whether by using the physicality of print to express concepts or by turning a location into a piece of typography.

→02 WARM: A Feminist Art Collective in Minnesota *exhibition catalog, 2007 (Author: Joanna Inglot; Client: Weisman Art Museum)*

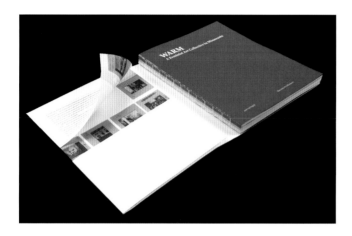

21 — Harriet Bart
The Processional (The Innocent, The Siren, The Matriarch, The Mourner, The Ancestor), 1977–78

MATTHEW REZAC

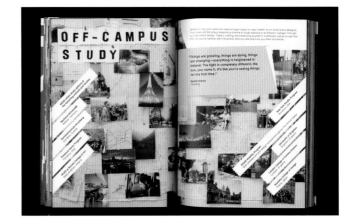

→03 *Spreads from* Become *catalog, 2007 (Designed with Alex DeArmond; Client: Minneapolis College of Art and Design [MCAD])*

↱04 *MCAD events calendar, 2008 (Client: Minneapolis College of Art and Design)*

This is not a book. This is an invitation, a container for unstable images, a model for further action. Here is the formula: Riley and his story. Me and my outrage. You and us.

Riley was a friend in college and later served as a nurse at Abu Ghraib prison. This is a container for Riley's digital pictures and fleeting traumatic memories. Images he could not fully secure or expel and entrusted to me.

Art can be a series of acts and challenges. Currently the artwork is an object in your hand — organized, mobile, tactile — a stable site to see information once elusive. The artist can mobilize information by provoking, listening, imagining, organizing and reorganizing. Right now, I am the artist. I want you to see what this war did to Riley.

Pay attention. This experience happens right in your lap. To make it happen, you must read compassionately, then actively. Then the experience happens wherever you take this container and whenever you respond to my invitation.

You and us, yes. Then you and another. This invitation is a model for veterans, families and friends to speak and share openly with each other. The artwork and artist are adaptable; you, the tactical reader, can use this object for your own device, or you can attend to another archive in need of careful attention. This is not a book. It is an object of deployment.

Riley and his story. *book, 2009 (Author: Monica Haller and Riley Sharbanno; Client: onestar press/Falth & Hassler)*

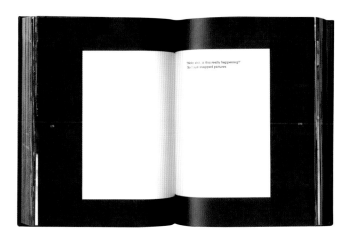

—— It seems to me that memories work on a few senses that are happening at the same time. You don't remember things because you experience them. You remember them because of some smell, some scent, music — something associated with the event. Then your mind connects all things together and creates a reality. For some events, I don't have any of those stored in my memory somehow. I can think back and smell the dust, or something like that, but that was always there and just the same every day. ——

MATTHEW REZAC

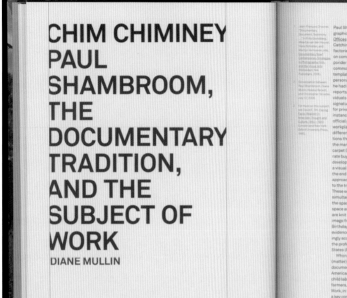

CHIM CHIMINEY PAUL SHAMBROOM, THE DOCUMENTARY TRADITION, AND THE SUBJECT OF WORK
DIANE MULLIN

Paul Shambroom's earliest cohesive photographic series, Factories (1986 – 88) and Offices (1989 – 90), focus on places of work. Catching glimpses of the spaces of industrial factories and corporate offices while working on commercial jobs, Shambroom began to ponder what interested him most about these common, almost clichéd, and generally uncontemplated environs. To delve into those more personal interests and responses to the spaces he had been portraying for corporate annual reports, he first used his connections to individuals in local businesses and honed his now signature letter-writing skills to arrange access for private shoots. Concentrating on the spaces, instances, and details never appropriate for official publications, his catalogue of American workplaces at the end of the 1980s tells a very different story from that told by the corporations themselves. From trivial details such as the mark left by a potted plant on a mundane carpet (Plate 14) to the aftermath of a corporate buyout (Plate 16), Shambroom started to develop in this early stage of his career both a visual lexicon of the American workplace at the end of the Reagan years and the unique approach that would become his contribution to the tradition of documentary photography. These early photographs not only reveal the simultaneously generic and chaotic nature of the spaces of work but also show how work space and work itself — even if begrudgingly — are knit tightly into American society. In one image from Offices, for instance, a "Happy 30th Birthday" balloon floats above cubicle walls, evidence of the somewhat uneasy but seemingly acceptable, even normative, blending of the professional and the personal in the United States (Plate 11).

When broadly considered, the subject (matter) of work emerges central in American documentary photography. The best-known American documentary images are Lewis Hine's child laborers and Dorothea Lange's migrant farmers, proving the importance of this topic. Work, in fact, is elemental to American life and a key component of the so-called American Dream, both an inherently good action and a means to the fabled "pursuit of happiness." Shambroom's Offices and Factories series

suggest that the importance of "work" (or "labor," to use a distinctly non-American term) may mean more than what is explicitly pictured. Though never his overt subject again, the idea and reality of work is at play in all of his major series, particularly in Meetings, in which he presents not only everyday labor but also the work of democracy in practice and that of the documentary photographer himself. With his "inside the whale" approach, Shambroom creates complex projects in familiar environments, photographs that are in the American documentary tradition as well as in the discourse of American democracy — as ideal and as practice.

There is a resounding chorus of agreement among photographers, historians, and critics that the term and even idea of "documentary photography" is without a solid and consistent basis. For some this marks a lack that cripples the practice and its discourse. For others, the ever-shifting definition is evidence of the field's strength and fluidity. In a recent essay on the documentary tradition and its current possibilities, Jean-François Chevrier begins, "The notion of documentary photography covers a variety of practices almost as wide as the idea of photography itself." Shambroom has weighed in on the notion of documentary and his relationship to the tradition and practice: "[documentary photographer] is a description that I've gone back and forth about feeling comfortable with. When I first started working as an artist I didn't really like the term...I thought it was limiting....But now that I am less of a documentary photographer, I'm more comfortable with it." "The problem of the lack of a definitive definition aside, or perhaps underlying, one can speak of a certain tradition of the documentary — both images and practice — at the center of American photography (and by extension American art since the mid-nineteenth century. This mode in American photography is based in a particularly American interest in facts and realism. In the United States facts and objectivity in social thought and art became paramount in the late nineteenth and into the twentieth centuries, contributing to the success and persistence of the documentary tradition in this country.

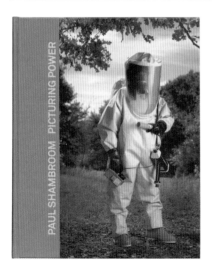

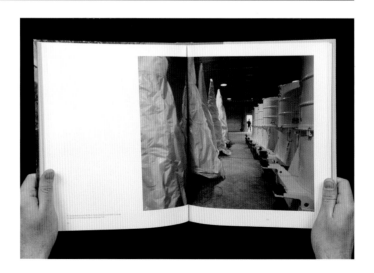

Paul Shambroom: Picturing Power book, 2008 (Designed with Andrew Blauvelt; Author: Paul Shambroom; Client: Weisman Art Museum)

Jay Heikes: Like a Broken Record exhibition announcement, 2007 (Client: Marianne Boesky Gallery)

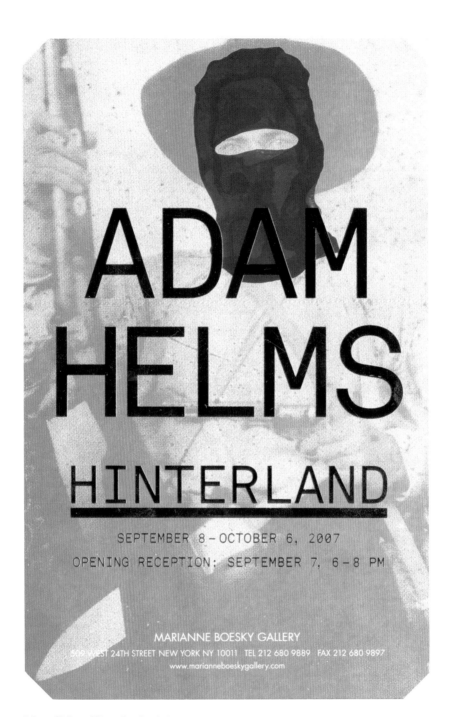

Adam Helms: Hinterland exhibition announcement, 2007
(Client: Marianne Boesky Gallery)

Donald Moffett
Easy Clean
Oct 11 – Nov 8 2008

Opening Oct 10 6 – 8 pm

MARIANNE BOESKY GALLERY
509 WEST 24TH STREET NEW YORK NY 10011 212 680 9889
www.marianneboeskygallery.com

Donald Moffett: Easy Clean exhibition announcement, 2008
(Client: Marianne Boesky Gallery)

SEA

For over a decade London-based SEA, the partnership of Bryan Edmondson and John Simpson has been making the hybrid of International Typographic Style design with high-end materials that is now de rigeur with a new generation of designers. SEA takes the crisp typography of late-sixties Swiss design and builds upon it with print effects—unusual papers, varnishes, or embossing—and stunning photography, resulting in a contemporary take on the International Typographic Style.

The most striking element of their work may be their use of materials, like the reflective metallic papers used in their catalogs and posters for The Architectural Foundation (London, 2001). →01 These projects utilize a familiar Swiss Typography, but their physical materiality emphasizes them as objects and plants them firmly in the present: for example, the use of reflective papers creates a shift in appearance determined by the position of the viewer. "SEA is all about design. Pure and Simple," declares the designers' website. For SEA, design is about objects—things to be handled and handed about. They create pieces that invite touch and reflection, and much of their work highlights the edges of a surface. The studio has worked with specialty papers manufacturer GF Smith (London) since 1999, and this relationship has allowed SEA to fully explore the physical element of design.

The *Colorplan* book (2002), showcasing a collection of colored stock, was inspired by the paper stacks in one of GF Smith's warehouses. →02 Typography plays a role in lending a physical dimension to the work—running throughout the pages is large Helvetica Neue type that always bleeds off the sides. Rather than the more obvious use of embossing and other print effects to exaggerate the physicality of the type, the letters have literally been chopped off. You can actually run your fingers along the exposed edge of the letter *e*.

While Helvetica Neue and Akzidenz Grotesk often appear in their work, there are those instances that call for a softer approach. The identity for British cafe

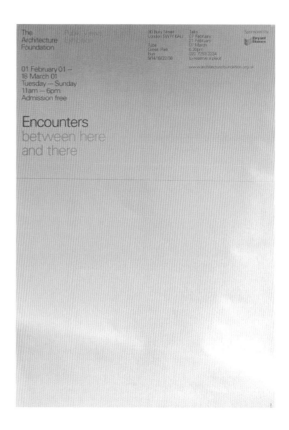

→01 *The Architecture Foundation collateral, 2001 (Client: The Architecture Foundation)* top *poster* bottom *exhibition catalogs*

→02 Colorplan *promotional book, 2002*
(Client: GF Smith)

SEA

s&m (for "sausage and mash") (2002) is a solely typographic solution based on onomatopoeia and lists, and the servers' T-shirts display a list of classic English food combinations set in stacks of Clarendon type. →03 Their mugs, meanwhile, are printed with words that suggest sounds of eating: dunk, slurp, sip, gulp. Coupled with the restaurant's retro interior, the effect is a demented take on all things classically British.

SEA has been on the path of designing using a clean, iconic, and Modern aesthetic for more than ten years. While some projects look as fresh now as when they were originally designed—the 1999 *Substance* exhibition catalog for GF Smith, for example—the s&m identity shows that their typographically bold solutions can be utilized in a multitude of ways. →04

→03 *s&m identity system, 2009 (Client: s&m)*

→04 Substance *exhibition catalog, 1999 (Author: Rankin; Client: GF Smith)*

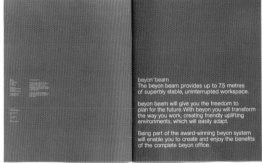

Beyon collateral, 2001–7 (Client: Beyon) left and top right *catalog* bottom right *poster*

SPIN

If there was one group working today that has truly maintained the trajectory of the sixties and seventies International Typographic Style, it is London-based Spin, founded by Patricia Finegan and Tony Brooks in 1992. While they are not dogmatic in their approach—they do not restrict themselves to sans-serif typefaces or a specific way of setting type—there is a simplicity in their work. They often solve their design problems typographically, through formal systems with a recurring Brutalist strain. Images rarely make an appearance—except in the case of work for galleries and museums in which reproductions of artworks are present.

The recent identity design for Fundación Proa (2008), a museum in Buenos Aires, uses a classic Modernist approach of distilling a prominent element of the institution into the main identity concept. In this instance Spin focused on the steel girders that feature prominently in the museum's new building from which they developed a custom typeface. →01 The application on the exhibition signage is a brash usage of the typeface at a single size, left justified, with the color of the type used to distinguish between the grouping of information. Artworks from the exhibitions are used on the posters as well, but ultimately the typeface is the dominant visual element. →02

Equally informed by a Modernist approach, but with a wholly different outcome, is the identity design for an on-going collaboration with Haunch of Venison, a contemporary art gallery in London. →03 Perhaps Spin's best-known work, the Haunch of Venison identity system (2002) is based on a grid of information and rule lines applied like a strip of tape to their print collateral. In the gallery's exhibition posters, the genius of the system comes to life. Each show is given its own visual identity, usually a bold combination of image and typography. The familiar strip is then laid on the right side of

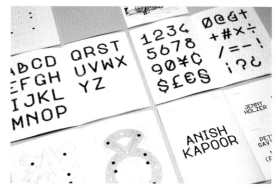

→01 *Fundación Proa exterior signage, 2008 (Client: Fundacion Proa)*

→02 *Fundación Proa gallery signage, 2008*
(Client: Fundacion Proa)

SPIN

the announcements, creating an instantly recognizable profile of Haunch of Venison while allowing each exhibition to retain its own identity. →04–07

Spin's greatest strength might be their ability to approach diverse contexts and audiences, resulting in playful and bright graphics for exhibitions like The Science Of →08 (The Science Museum, London, 2007), and more traditional typography for the grocery chain Sainsbury's →09 & 10 (2009). In each of these cases, they created work that captures the individuality of the subject without losing sight of their own design methodology.

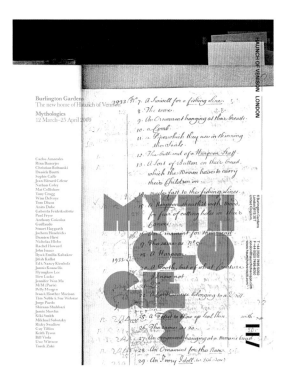

→03 *Mythologies exhibition advertisement overlaid with the Haunch of Venison identity system, 2009 (Client: Haunch of Venison)*

→04 *Mythologies exhibition, 2009 (Client: Haunch of Venison)*
top *wall graphics* bottom row *catalog*

Dan Flavin Works from the 1960s exhibition, 2005 (Client: Haunch of Venison) above *window graphics* opposite *poster*

DAN
FLAVIN
WORKS
FROM
THE
1960S

6 Haunch of Venison Yard
off Brook Street
London W1K 5ES
England

T +44 (0) 20 7495 5050
F +44 (0) 20 7495 4050
info@haunchofvenison.com
www.haunchofvenison.com

Exhibition dates
12/02—16/03/2005

the diagonal of May 25 1963
1963
Red fluorescent light
96in/244cm
© Stephen Flavin / DACS,
London

SPIN

→06 *Assorted Haunch of Venison exhibition announcements, 2002–9*
(Client: Haunch of Venison)

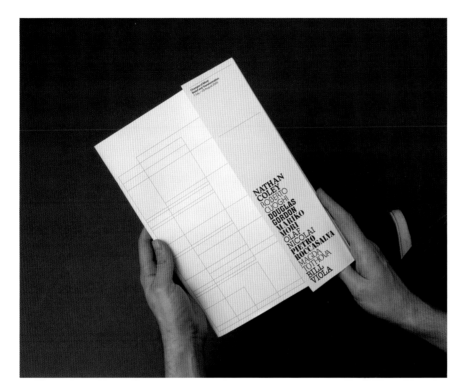

left Changes of Mind *exhibition catalog, 2005 (Author/Client: Haunch of Venison)*

top right Keith Tyson: Nature Paintings *exhibition catalog, 2008 (Author: Keith Tyson; Client: Haunch of Venison)*

bottom right Zhang Huan: Ash *exhibition catalog, 2007 (Author: Zhang Huan, Philip Tinari, Nina Miall; Client: Haunch of Venison)*

SPIN

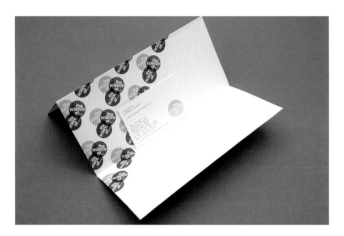

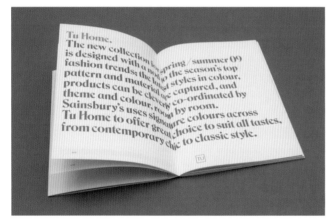

→08 top left *The Science Of identity system, 2007*
(Client: The Science Museum)

→09 *bottom left and right* *Spring/summer 2009*
collection catalog, 2009 (Client: Sainsbury's)

→10 *Spring/summer 2009 collection invitation, 2009 (Client: Sainsbury's)*

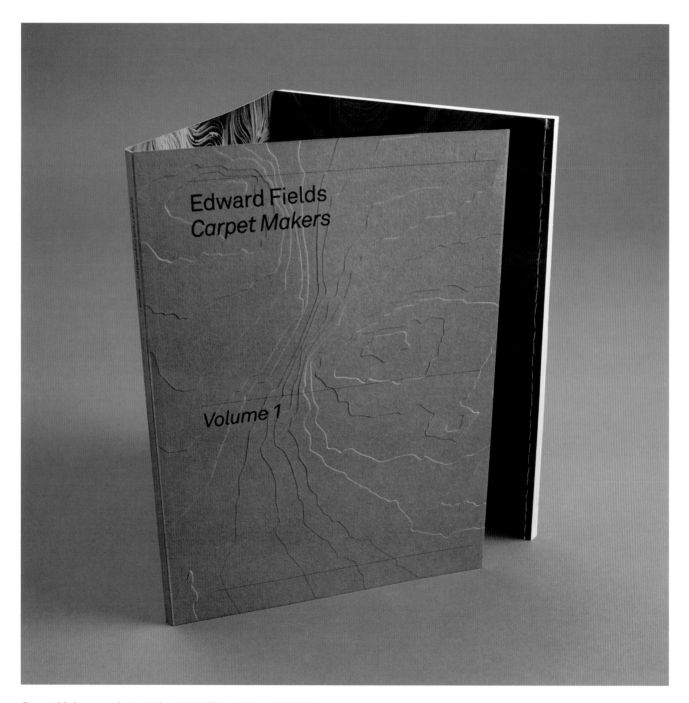

Carpet Makers *product catalog, 2008 (Client: Edward Fields)*

Locations

STUDIO TEMP

One can trace the development of a new typography by looking at the work of Studio Temp, an Italian design firm founded in 2007 by Fausto Giliberti, Guido Gregorio Daminelli, and Marco Fasolini. The designers' early works were classic examples of the new Techno Modernism, which is best exemplified by the visually dense fields of graphs, information, and minutiae found in the work of designer Michael C. Place of Build (formerly of The Designers Republic). The publication *A/B* (2007) explores the role of music in the designers' lives from 1984 to 2006 by contrasting each year's top pop song with the designers' favorites of the year, which they call the "B-Sides." For example, in 1984 Michael Jackson's "Thriller," the A-Side, is paired with the punk band Hüsker Dü's "Height Mile High," the B-Side. →01 The real point of the project was to use the songs, or rather the data associated with the songs—time codes, sound waves, and album-release information—as a jumping-off point for their Helvetica Neue–driven information design. Every fact that could be extrapolated was pulled out to create a book dense with the texture of info-graphics.

12/13 (2008) was created in a workshop on bookmaking led by art director Giacomo Gabriele Callo at Politecnico di Milano (Milan). Studio Temp used the information related to the workshop—dates, locations, and credits—as content for a book about the workshop. With only bare-bones data to communicate, Studio Temp created an artist's book that looks like graphic design. →02 Works like *A/B* and *12/13*, with their hyperdetailed level of information—page dimensions and units of measure as content—helped Studio Temp to hone the level of craft and restraint that would define their later work.

More recently, the designers have explored a more diverse aesthetic incorporating elements of Classical typography while gradually shedding information-based ornamentation. *CTRL* magazine (2009) retains their attention to detail and typographic hierarchy

→01 A/B *book, 2007 (Client: self-published)*

STUDIO TEMP

but is marked by a more eccentric use of typefaces and layouts that often fill the pages from edge to edge. →03 The on-going broadsheet arts journal *Peep-Hole Sheet* (2009) is even more stripped down than *CTRL* but may be their boldest work. →04 Each issue consists of a writing by a single artist, and the sheer scale of the format seems to be something of an homage to the artist. The paper color alternates between white and neon, creating striking visual shifts. The text-heavy center spread is preceded and followed by pages with only the artist's first and last names, respectively, to dramatic effect.

Their identity and accompanying catalog *Phobia Paper* for the group exhibition The Fear Society (The Venice Biennale, Venice, 2009) revisits some of the same strategies used in *CTRL*—the use of centered type, idiosyncratic fonts, and a bold Brutalist tone—but added an interesting handling of photography cast informally on the pages. →05 & 06 In some ways it feels as though the techniques applied for informational detailing in *A/B* or *12/13* are now being used with photography. This is not to say that those gestures of information-driven design are completely gone, but what was once an almost ornamental use of typography that relegated information to texture, rather than something to be communicated, is now a navigational element. In earlier works, the running indicia would likely have been set at eight points and more likely to create information overload than be useful. The Fear Society type is set at a more reader-friendly size that is actually a bit bigger than the text typeface.

→02 12/13 *book, 2008 (Author: Studio Temp; Client: self-published)*

STUDIO TEMP

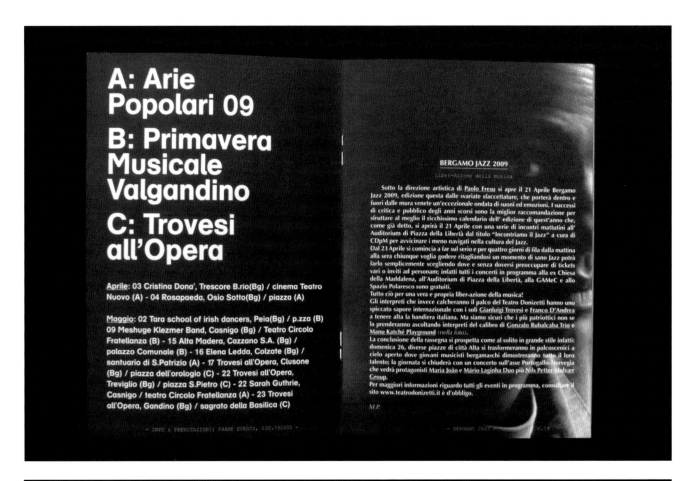

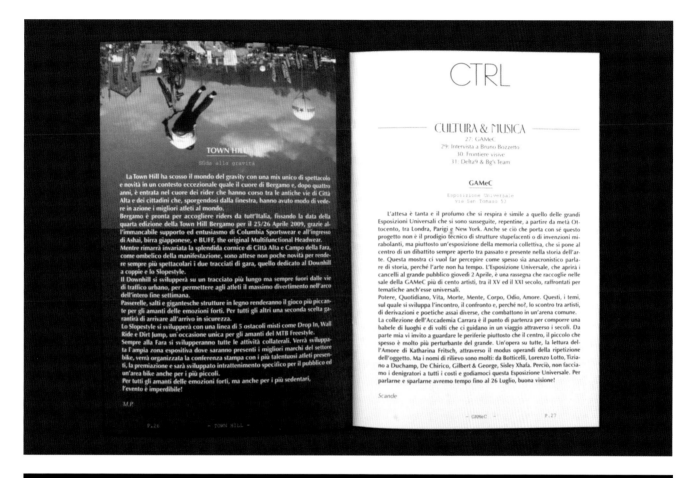

TOWN HILL
Sfida alla gravità

La Town Hill ha scosso il mondo del gravity con una mix unico di spettacolo e novità in un contesto eccezionale quale il cuore di Bergamo e, dopo quattro anni, è entrata nel cuore dei rider che hanno corso tra le antiche vie di Città Alta e dei cittadini che, sporgendosi dalla finestra, hanno avuto modo di vedere in azione i migliori atleti al mondo.

Bergamo è pronta per accogliere riders da tutt'Italia, fissando la data della quarta edizione della Town Hill Bergamo per il 25/26 Aprile 2009, grazie all'immancabile supporto ed entusiasmo di Columbia Sportswear e all'ingresso di Ashai, birra giapponese, e BUFF, the original Multifunctional Headwear.

Mentre rimarrà invariata la splendida cornice di Città Alta e Campo della Fara, come ombelico della manifestazione, sono attese non poche novità per rendere sempre più spettacolari i due tracciati di gara, quello dedicato al Downhill a coppie e lo Slopestyle.

Il Downhill si svilupperà su un tracciato più lungo ma sempre fuori dalle vie di traffico urbano, per permettere agli atleti il massimo divertimento nell'arco dell'intero fine settimana.

Passerelle, salti e gigantesche strutture in legno renderanno il gioco più piccante per gli amanti delle emozioni forti. Per tutti gli altri una seconda scelta garantirà di arrivare all'arrivo in sicurezza.

Lo Slopestyle si svilupperà con una linea di 5 ostacoli misti come Drop In, Wall Ride e Dirt Jump, un'occasione unica per gli amanti del MTB Freestyle.

Sempre alla Fara si svilupperanno tutte le attività collaterali. Verrà sviluppata l'ampia zona espositiva dove saranno presenti i migliori marchi del settore bike, verrà organizzata la conferenza stampa con i più talentuosi atleti presenti, la premiazione e sarà sviluppato intrattenimento specifico per il pubblico ed un'area bike anche per i più piccoli.

Per tutti gli amanti delle emozioni forti, ma anche per i più sedentari, l'evento è imperdibile!

M.P.

P.26   — TOWN HILL —

CTRL

CULTURA & MUSICA
27. GAMeC
29: Intervista a Bruno Bozzetto
30: Frontiere visive
31: Delta9 & Bg's Team

GAMeC
Esposizione Universale
Via San Tomaso 53

L'attesa è tanta e il profumo che si respira è simile a quello delle grandi Esposizioni Universali che si sono susseguite, repentine, a partire dalla metà Ottocento, tra Londra, Parigi e New York. Anche se ciò che porta con sé questo progetto non è il prodigio tecnico di strutture stupefacenti o di invenzioni mirabolanti, ma piuttosto un'esposizione della memoria collettiva, che si pone al centro di un dibattito sempre aperto tra passato e presente nella storia dell'arte. Questa mostra ci vuol far percepire come spesso sia anacronistico parlare di storia, perché l'arte non ha tempo. L'Esposizione Universale, che aprirà i cancelli al grande pubblico giovedì 2 Aprile, è una rassegna che raccoglie nelle sale della GAMeC più di cento artisti, tra il XV ed il XXI secolo, raffrontati per tematiche anch'esse universali.

Potere, Quotidiano, Vita, Morte, Mente, Corpo, Odio, Amore. Questi, i temi, sul quale si sviluppa l'incontro, il confronto e, perché no?, lo scontro tra artisti, di derivazioni e poetiche assai diverse, che combattono in un'arena comune. La collezione dell'Accademia Carrara è il punto di partenza per comporre una babele di luoghi e di volti che ci guidano in un viaggio attraverso i secoli. Da parte mia vi invito a guardare le periferie piuttosto che il centro, il piccolo che spesso è molto più perturbante del grande. Un'opera su tutte, la lettura dell'Amore di Katharina Fritsch, attraverso il modus operandi della ripetizione dell'oggetto. Ma i nomi di rilievo sono molti: da Botticelli, Lorenzo Lotto, Tiziano a Duchamp, De Chirico, Gilbert & George, Sisley Xhafa. Perciò, non facciamo i denigratori a tutti i costi e godiamoci questa Esposizione Universale. Per parlarne e sparlarne avremo tempo fino al 26 Luglio, buona visione!

Scande

— GAMeC —   P.27

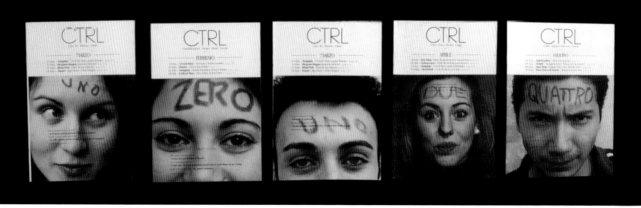

STUDIO TEMP

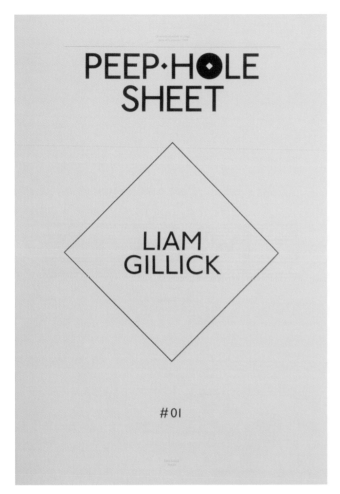

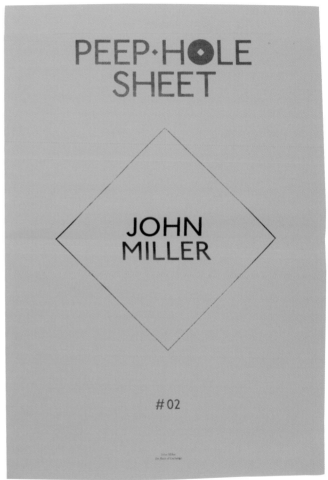

→04 Peep-Hole Sheet *magazine, 2009 (Client: Mousse Publishing)*

STUDIO TEMP

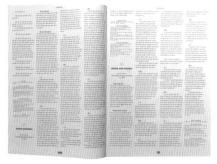

→05 Phobia Paper *exhibition catalog for* The Fear Society, *2009 (Client: Mousse Publishing)*

A] **Tania Bruguera** · Tatlin Workshop, 2007, use of psychology techniques, Ex-KGB agent, street photographers, eagles, monkeys, photographic paper, printer, ink, photo of Felix Dzerzhinsky, 4 × 3 × 2 m. Courtesy the artist and 2nd Moscow Biennial. Photo: 2nd Moscow Biennial B] **Joao Castro** · Untitled 2, 2009, installation, 40 m-brada sticks, each 480 cm long. Courtesy the artist and Galerie Barbara Thumm, Berlin C] **Fernando Bryce** · Die Welt, 2008, series of 195 drawings, ink on paper, variable dimensions. Courtesy the artist and Galerie Barbara Thumm, Berlin D] **Alfredo Jaar** · Un Cierto de Pasolini, 2009, still from video. Courtesy the artist and Galleria Lia Rumma, Milan E] **Jesús Martines Oliva** · Cuadrículas y rollos, 2009, collage, 39 × 42 cm. Courtesy the artist F] **Ami-Sofi Sidén** · Some Unknown Errant 1, 2009, 9-channel synced video installation, HD, 9 monitors, speakers, metal pole. Courtesy the artist and Galerie Barbara Thumm, Berlin G] **Hans Haacke** · West Bank 1994–27th Year of Occupation, 2007/2009, 2 text panels, 1 photo panel. Courtesy the artist © Hans Haacke/VG Bild-Kunst H] **Rainer Ganahl** · Izmir NY / Credit Crunch 2009, paint on Tshirt... Izmir NY · Bernard Madoff 2009, paint on Tshirt. Courtesy the artist, Fruit and Flower Deli, New York and Elaine Lévy, Brussels I] **goldiechiari** · Genealogia di Dantastic Memories, 2009, carved magnolia. Courtesy the artist J] **Martin Dammann** · Soldier Studies / Dance 2007, jet print on aluminium, 52 × 75 cm · Soldier Studies · Slow Waltz 2007, jet print on aluminium, 73 × 54 cm; · Soldier Studies / Little Skirts 2, 2007, jet print on aluminium, 52 × 75 cm. Courtesy the artist, Burger Collection, Honk Hong / Switzerland and Galerie Barbara Thumm, Berlin K] **Jesus Segura** · Transported, 2007, 2-channel video installation. Courtesy the artist L] **Regina José Galindo** · Confession, 2007, performance, Caja Blanca, Palma de Mallorca. Photo: Julian Stokabratos. Courtesy prometeogallery, Milan/Lucca

STUDIO TEMP

→06 The Fear Society *exhibition guide, 2009 (Author: The Fear Society;*
Client: Comunidad Autónoma de la Región de Murcia)

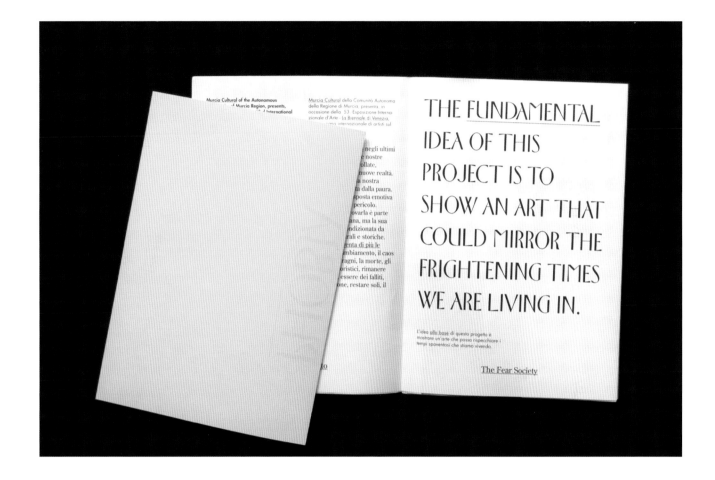

THE FUNDAMENTAL
IDEA OF THIS
PROJECT IS TO
SHOW AN ART THAT
COULD MIRROR THE
FRIGHTENING TIMES
WE ARE LIVING IN.

L'idea alla base di questo progetto è
mostrare un'arte che possa rispecchiare i
tempi spaventosi che stiamo vivendo.

The Fear Society

STUDIO TEMP

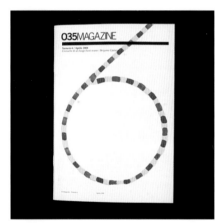

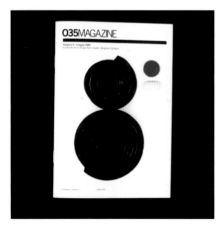

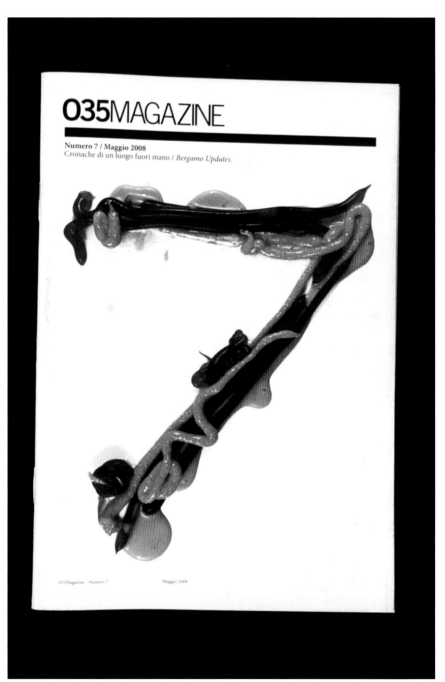

035 Magazine, *2008 (Client: 035 Magazine)*

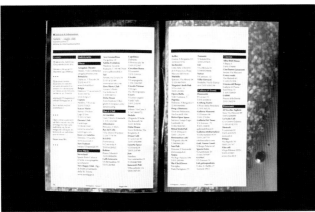

WALKER ART CENTER

The in-house design studio at the Walker Art Center has long been an innovative force in design, whether by spreading European Modernism to the Midwest in the sixties—under the direction of Peter Seitz—or by putting the Postmodernist theory of nineties academia into practical application through the work of Laurie Haycock-Makela. Since 1998 the studio has been led by design director Andrew Blauvelt.

While there is an identity system in place for their institutional communications, there is no single design philosophy at the Walker, nor is there a house style. A design educator before joining the Walker, Blauvelt thinks of the studio as a classroom or laboratory, and this is reflected in the visual and conceptual diversity of materials produced by the studio's designers.[1] Nonetheless, the Walker has been a leading influence in the United States in the movement toward a cleaner typography over the past decade.

A 2007 poster announcing their annual design fellowship shows the prominent role of typography in the work of the designers: it displays the dominant type elements from more than fifty projects completed by the current design fellows. →01 Not only does it display their range but also the attention to detail given to even the smallest of projects (e.g., signage for a closed gallery). Furthermore, the conceptual clarity of the studio shows through in the direct nature of the composition—each element is reproduced in its original colors, with no attempt to unify the forms beyond a grid. The headline is a simple and unadorned solution—a red box with white Times New Roman type laid on top of the design.

For the exhibition Andy Warhol/Supernova: Stars, Deaths, and Disasters, 1962–1964 (2005), the pop artist's iconic screen prints are transformed into typographic symbols. →02 & 03 A painting of Marilyn Monroe is interpreted as a yellow MARILYN on a turquoise field. Each item in the campaign is a bold distillation of Warhol's own Brutalist repetition. The tightly kerned Franklin Gothic seems so much

All works designed for the
Walker Art Center.

→01 *Design Fellowship poster, 2007*

→02 *Andy Warhol/Supernova: Stars, Deaths, and Disasters, 1962–1964 billboard, 2005*

of Warhol's time that these new type "paintings" feel familiar, like some forgotten pieces of the artist's oeuvre.

The studio explores language, conventions, and the interconnectedness of print and web in a poster series for the 2009 Insights lecture series, a program cocurated by the Walker and AIGA Minnesota. →04 Each designer was asked a series of non-design-related questions. The posters reveal the answers to these questions and direct the viewer to the studio's blog for the questions. Each poster follows a strict system, and when they are viewed together, they form a kind of info-graphic of each designer's responses. Eric Olson and Nicole Dotin of Process Type Foundry answer in a conversational tone and results in the longest text of the four interviews, while David Reinfurt gives a short, one-paragraph response. The uniqueness of each responder's personality is visible before you even begin to read.

Most institutions typically use their communications as headlines and demands, not as prompts and questions, as the Walker does. But the influence the Walker has in both the art and design world is clear and is evidence that design can be experimental and still retain the ability to communicate with its audience.

NOTES

1. Andrew Blauvelt, interview with author, 2009.

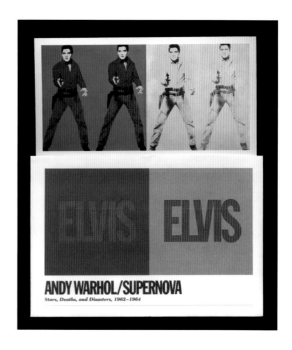

→03 *Andy Warhol/Supernova exhibition identity system, 2005* above and opposite bottom left *exhibition announcements* opposite top row *catalog (Editor: Douglas Fogle)* opposite bottom right *poster*

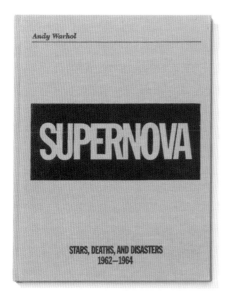

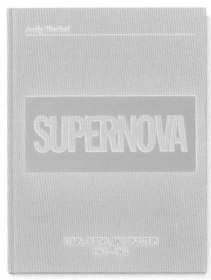

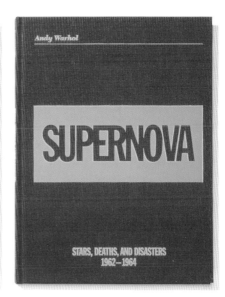

Process Type Foundry,
Tuesday, March 10, 7 pm   Eric Olson & Nicole Dotin

O-R-G &
Tuesday, March 17, 7 pm   David Reinfurt

Dexter Sinister, Experimental
Tuesday, March 24, 7 pm   Marieke Stolk & Danny van den Dungen

Jetset, Ellen
Tuesday, March 31, 7 pm   Ellen Lupton

Lupton.

Avant la lettre: Insights 2009 Design Lecture Series
March 10–31
Walker Art Center

The Walker Art Center and AIGA Minnesota (minnesota.aiga.org) present Insights,
a lecture series that brings graphic designers from across the country and around the world to the Twin Cities.
Series tickets: $70 ($48 AIGA/Walker members)   Individual event tickets: $20 ($15; $10 students)
Tickets/Information: 612.375.7600   walkerart.org/tickets

A David Reinfurt: I'm really not sure how to respond as all the questions assume some sort of break in time, before and after. Although I do understand that things happen in an order, I typically can only make sense of it as one thing. C-o-n-t-i-n-u-o-u-s and  c,o,n,n,e,c,t,e,d.

&

Q blogs.walkerart.org/design

→04 Insights lecture series posters, 2009

Eric Olson: Coalesce, MC5, Converge, Fabric, The Faces, and John Adams. Nicole Dotin: I think I'm still listening to it. EO: I don't have any heroes. ND: I am inspired by the exceptional actions of others, but I don't have any heroines. EO: Fear, I suppose. Mostly of speaking in public and driving through intersections. ND: If I was obsessed with anything, it would have been perfection . . . and I still haven't learned any better. EO: To become a type designer. ND: To find what fit. EO: Robin Kinross and Jonathan Franzen come to mind. ND: A lot of American history at the time of the Revolution. EO: I don't collect. ND: I've never had a collector's mentality for objects, but I've always collected skills because I've always loved to learn. EO: A teacher, freelance graphic designer, office temp, and construction laborer. ND: A typography teacher, graphic designer, Web designer, and seamstress/tailor.

blogs.walkerart.org/design

Walker Art Center
1750 Hennepin Avenue
Minneapolis, MN 55403
walkerart.org

Nonprofit Organization
U.S. Postage
PAID
Minneapolis, MN
Permit Number 5213

©2009 Walker Art Center

Paper are printing.com/blogs
Sexton Printing, Inc., Minneapolis

WALKER ART CENTER

Walker Art Center
Annual Report 2005–2006

-771-
Artists

771 Artists: Walker Art Center Annual
Report 2005–2006, *2006*

House of Oracles: A Huang Yong Ping Retrospective *book, 2005*
(Editor: Philippe Vergne and Doryun Chong)

WALKER ART CENTER

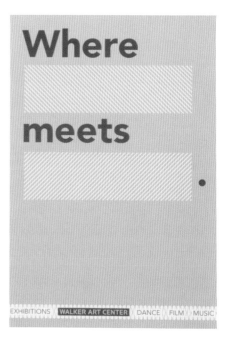

Walker Art Center expansion opening campaign identity system, 2005
top row **postcards** bottom **T-shirt** opposite **poster**

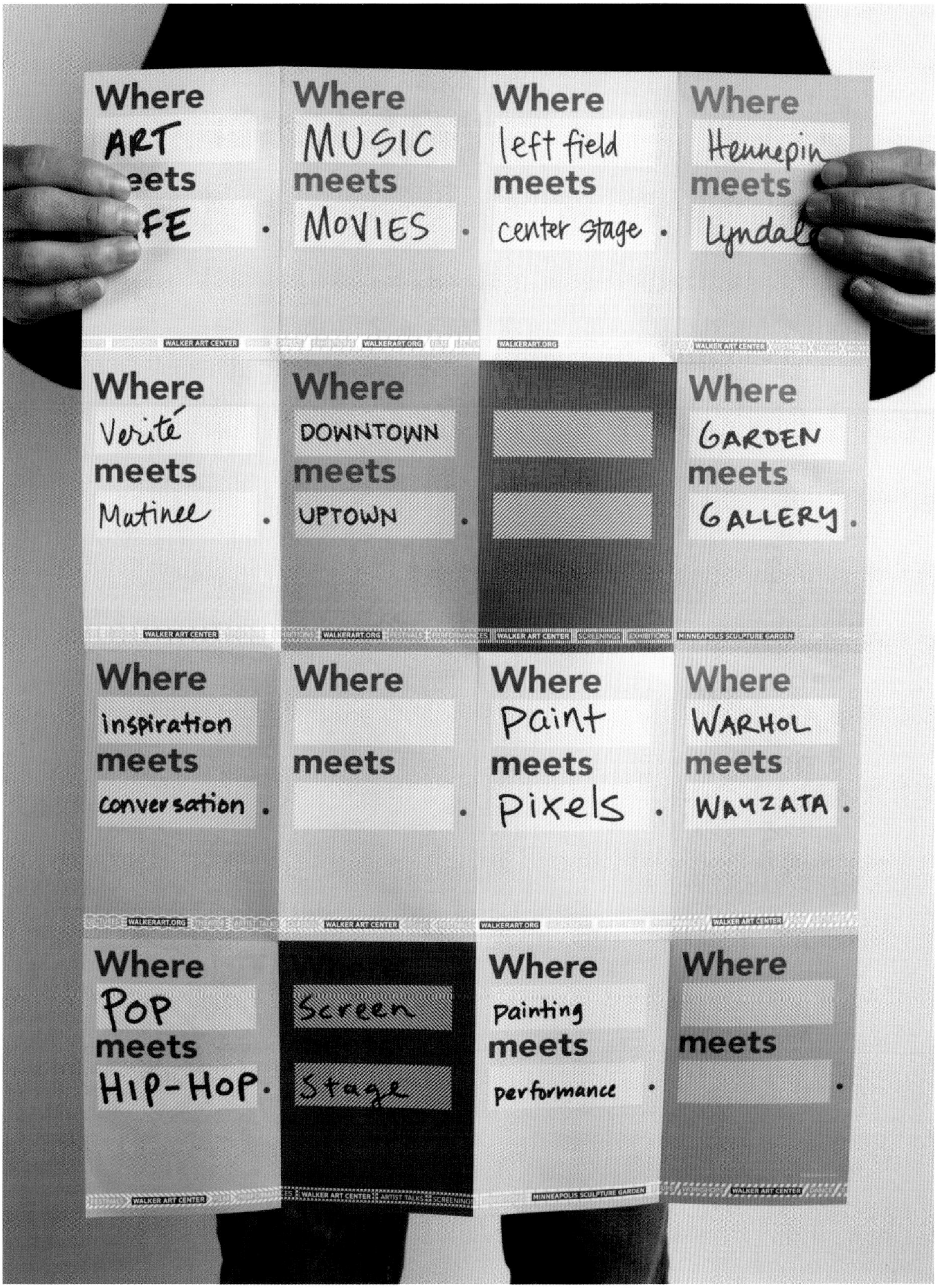

Where ART
Where MUSIC meets MOVIES.
Where left field meets center stage.
Where Hennepin
Where Verité meets Matinee.
Where DOWNTOWN meets UPTOWN.
Where GARDEN meets GALLERY.
Where inspiration meets conversation.
Where meets .
Where Paint meets pixels.
Where WARHOL meets WAYZATA.
Where POP meets HIP-HOP.
Screen
Stage
Where Painting meets performance.
Where meets .
WALKER ART CENTER
WALKERART.ORG
MINNEAPOLIS SCULPTURE GARDEN
SCREENINGS
EXHIBITIONS
FESTIVALS
PERFORMANCES
ARTIST TALKS
THEATER
WORKSHOPS

> **Dear you hypocritical fucking Twerp,**
>
> Id just like to thank you for taking hold of the last four years of my life and raising my hopes for the future. Id like to thank you for giving me clothes when I needed them and food when I needed it and for fucking my brains out when my brains needed fucking. I hope that the time we spent in the Quarters with my family sleeping neerby quietly ignoring what you proceeded to do to me— what, rather I proceeded to do to you—

Kara Walker: My Complement, My Enemy, My Oppressor, My Love *book, 2007*
(Author: Kara Walker)

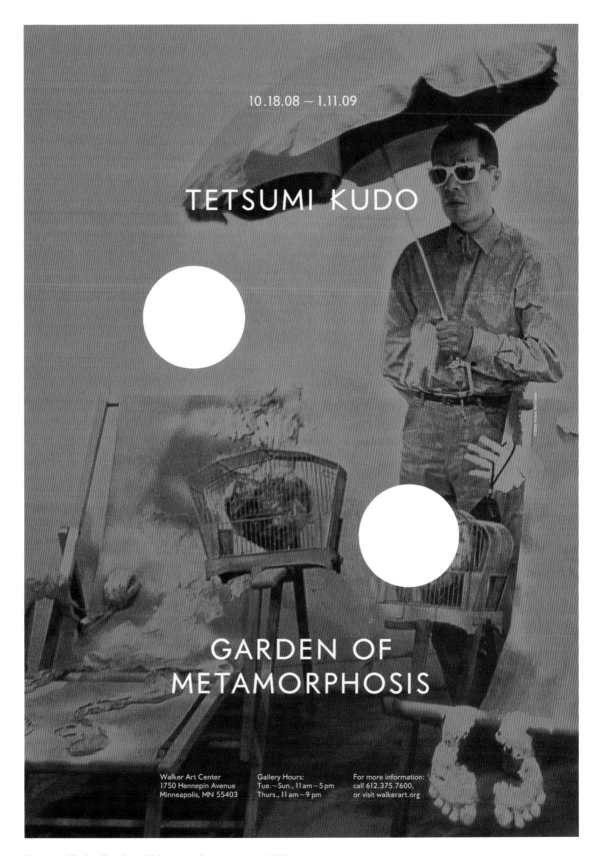

Tetsumi Kudo: Garden of Metamorphosis poster, 2008

JOHN WIESE

John Wiese is an experimental musician who has
been prolifically releasing records on his own label,
Helicopter, as well as dozens of other labels, since
1998, often in extremely limited editions—one record
was issued with only eleven copies. The design of
Wiese's records is in direct contrast to the dominant
aesthetic of the "noise" music scene that he operates
in, which tends toward the "transgressive"—black-
and-white imagery of war, horror-film stills, and
an obsession with violence. In addition to the fact
that the sleeves have no identifying genre affiliations,
Wiese's releases look noticeably designed—custom
typefaces, inventive formats, sophisticated typography.
When imagery was used, it possessed an ephemeral,
abstract, sketchlike quality. It isn't surprising that
Wiese is a practicing graphic designer with a degree
from CalArts in Los Angeles.

    Present throughout Wiese's work is an understated
use of typography—if not the only visual element—
that often takes a backseat to the illustrations he
commissions. Like the work of Norwegian designer
Kim Hiorthøy for the Rune Grammofon record label,
Wiese's designs reveal how the most exciting music
packaging usually originates from a personal response
to the music rather than from a desire to use the
visual graphic language of a specific genre. (The most
oft-cited example of the former might be the genre-
defining work of Reid Miles for the jazz label Blue
Note. Miles famously disliked jazz and sold off his
own personal collection of valuable Blue Note records
that he acquired while designing for the label. His
designs that have come to epitomize the jazz aesthetic
were the combination of his own instincts about the
music and the notes that Blue Note founder Francis
Wolff would share with him.)

    The prolific nature of Wiese's musical output
(he appears as artist, guest musician, or remixer on
over three hundred releases in the last ten years)
in a genre where creative control is sacrosanct has
allowed him the opportunity to freely experiment

Heat Directors
Volume 1

Mitchell Brown — David Kendall — Damion Romero — John Wiese

H 32

→01 Heat Directors Volume 1 *7" record, 2004 (Artists:
Various; Client: Helicopter)*

→02 New York/Atlanta *LP, 2008*
(Artists: John Wiese and C. Spencer Yeh; Client: Helicopter)

JOHN WIESE

as a designer, exploring multiple themes simultaneously. As a result, it is difficult to pin down his style, but one trend that has emerged over the last few years is an increasing number of purely typographic sleeves with Classical typographic sensibility. The most obvious example of this is the sleeve for Dave Phillips and John Wiese's seven-inch *At A Loss For Words* (2006), which is letterpressed and carries some of the same somber weight as early Peter Saville sleeves for Factory Records, and the *Heat Directors Volume 1* seven-inch (2004). →01 The more Modern-looking pieces, such as John Wiese & C. Spencer Yeh's *New York/Atlanta* LP (2008), also display a restraint that allows a timelessness to emerge in the designs. →02

This difficulty of identifying a single aesthetic at any one point is one of the most exciting parts of watching Wiese's development. While he will likely continue to pursue the restrained typography used on Sissy Spacek's *Glass* CD (2009), he will still continue to create contrasting designs such as the hair lettering of the *Hair Stylistics & John Wiese* LP (2010) and the patterned typography of Sissy Spacek's *California Axe* box set (2009). →03–05

→03 Glass *CD, 2009 (Artist: Sissy Spacek; Client: Misanthropic Agenda)*

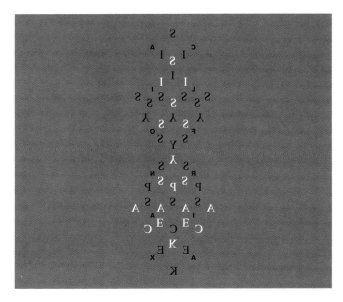

SISSY SPACEK 13-TET

Mitchell Brown
Kate Hall
Joeseph Hammer
Aaron Hemphill
Tim Koh
Giles Miller
Damion Romero
Corydon Ronnau
Jarrett Silberman
Dean Spunt
David Scott Stone
Shannon Walter
John Wiese

Sissy Spacek 13-Tet:
Mitchell Brown, Percussion
Kate Hall, Percussion
Joeseph Hammer, Tape
Aaron Hemphill, Guitar
Tim Koh, Percussion
Giles Miller, Woodwinds
Damion Romero, Electronics
Corydon Ronnau, Guitar
Jarrett Silberman, Guitar
Dean Spunt, Percussion
David Scott Stone, Electronics
Shannon Walter, Electronics
John Wiese, Electronics

Thursday,
December 13th, 2007
At The Smell
Doors At 9pm
Two Sets At 10pm & 11pm
$5, All Ages
The Smell
247 South Main Street
Downtown Los Angeles
myspace.com/thesmell
More Information:
gorejet.com
john-wiese.com
johnwiese@earthlink.net

→04 top left Hair Stylistics & John Wiese
*LP, 2010 (Artists: Hair Stylistics and
John Wiese; Client: Helicopter)*

→05 bottom left California Axe
*box set, 2009 (Artist: Sissy Spacek;
Client: Helicopter)*

right *Sissy Spacek 13-Tet flyer, 2009
(Client: Sissy Spacek)*

JOHN WIESE

Country and Western CD, 2010 (Artists: Lasse Marhaug and John Wiese; Client: Helicopter)

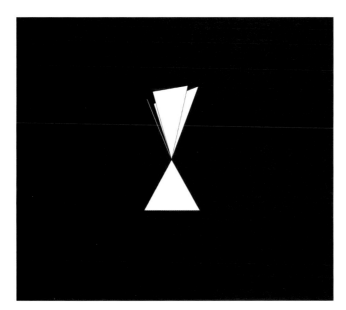

*Remote Whale Control CD, 2009 (Artist: Sissy Spacek;
Client: Misanthropic Agenda)* left *front cover* right *back cover*

YES

The London-based studio YES formed in 2004 by founder Simon Earith. The studio website states that it creates "commercial art," the term once used to describe what we now call graphic design. This is a clue to the direct, bold, and highly crafted work they produce.

The extreme simplicity of their work, whether record sleeves for bands or exhibition collateral for contemporary art galleries, may be in part a reaction to the flashy, surface-oriented nature of much of contemporary design that often celebrates trend-driven visuals over ideas. YES's work is often pared down to one or two elements, with none of the flashiness or "luxe simplicity" of agency work. Earith describes YES as "lapsed Modernists...influenced by Modernism's ideals and reductive language, but not restricted to a single aesthetic or methodology." The identity program for arts organization A Foundation (London and Liverpool) uses bold Helvetica in a Brutalist manner to brand its communications. →01 The centered placement of the huge type shares more with the undesigned qualities of leftist political pamphlets of the seventies than the current obsession with Helvetica and grids.

When YES makes Modernist-looking work, it looks past the stylistic details and searches for a more basic core aesthetic. Their redesign of four books from the Penguin Modern Classics series—*On Photography*, *Ways of Seeing*, *The Medium Is The Message*, and *Design As Art* (all from 2008)—is clearly influenced by the company's design legacy, but much of the obvious Penguin details—the Helvetica Neue, rule lines, and the famous Marber Grid developed by Romek Marber in 1961 for the Penguin Crime series—have all been replaced by an extreme unadorned minimalism. →02 As a result, the series identity creates an alternate history—as if YES dug into the Penguin archives and found some unused first editions that were too radical in its bold simplicity to have actually been published during its time.

→01 A Bulletin *magazine, 2006 (Client: A Foundation)*

→02 *From the* Penguin on Design *book series, 2008 (Client: Penguin)*

YES

The studio has successfully brought their approach to the world of record cover design on multiple occasions. Their work for Maxïmo Park's *A Certain Trigger* album features a custom typeface created for the band, and the campaign for each album plays off a simple, but equally important, interplay between rigid Brutalist type and freeform, figurative photography. →03 By using one-color, high-contrast photography, the type is able to take a stronger role in the compositions, often acting as an anchor for the imagery.

Earith mentions Jan Tschichold as being an "enduring reference point[1]." Tschichold's stripped-down Classical typography came about as he was leaving the Modernist New Typography that he helped to innovate. Though he formally renounced the New Typography, his focus on reduction, function, and white space as a Modernist typographer reshaped his aesthetic, and when he returned to Classical book typography in 1949, he brought with him a more sparse and visually balanced approach to traditional typography. The most extreme examples of YES's Minimalist design recall Tschichold's later work in that it is stripped down to the barest essentials but designed with the skills learned from more complex past work.

NOTES

1. Simon Earith, interview with the author, 2009.

→03 A Certain Trigger *LP, 2005*
(Artist: Maxïmo Park; Client: Warp Records)

THE ANIMALS
THE ART OF NOISE
THE ASSOCIATION
THE B52'S
THE BAND
THE BEACH BOYS
THE BEATLES
THE BIRTHDAY PARTY
THE BLUE NILE
THE BOX TOPS
THE BUZZCOCKS
THE BYRDS
THE CARS
THE CLASH
THE CRAMPS
THE COMMODORES
THE CORTINAS
THE CULT
THE CURE
THE DAMNED
THE DOORS
THE DRIFTERS
THE DURUTTI COLUMN
THE EVERLY BROTHERS
THE FACES
THE FALL
THE FOUNDATIONS
THE FATBACK BAND
THE FLAMING LIPS
THE FLYING BURRITO BROTHERS
THE FOUR TOPS
THE GRATEFUL DEAD
THE HEPTONES

THE HUMAN LEAGUE
THE IMPRESSIONS
THE INCREDIBLE STRING BAND
THE ISLEY BROTHERS
THE JAM
THE JACKSON 5
THE JB'S
THE JESUS AND MARY CHAIN
THE KINKS
THE KLF
THE LA'S
THE LOUNGE LIZARDS
THE LOVIN' SPOONFUL
THE MAMAS & THE PAPAS
THE MC5
THE MEKONS
THE METERS
THE MIRACLES
THE MODERN LOVERS
THE MONOCHROME SET
THE NEVILLE BROTHERS
THE O' JAYS
THE ONLY ONES
THE POGUES
THE POLICE
THE POP GROUP
THE PRETENDERS
THE PSYCHEDELIC FURS
THE RAMONES
THE RED KRAYOLA
THE RESIDENTS
THE ROLLING STONES
THE RONETTES

THE RUTS
THE SABRES OF PARADISE
THE SEEDS
THE SKATALITES
THE SKIDS
THE SLITS
THE SMITHS
THE SONICS
THE SPECIALS
THE SPINNERS
THE STRANGLERS
THE STRAY CATS
THE STONE ROSES
THE STOOGES
THE STYLE COUNCIL
THE SUGARCUBES
THE SUGARHILL GANG
THE SUPREMES
THE SWEET
THE TEARDROP EXPLODES
THE TEMPTATIONS
THE THE
THE TROGGS
THE TUBES
THE UNDERTONES
THE UPSETTERS
THE VELVET UNDERGROUND
THE WAILERS
THE WEDDING PRESENT
THE WHO
THE WILD BUNCH
THE YARDBIRDS
THE ZOMBIES

THE LIST

The List poster, 2005 (Client: self-published)

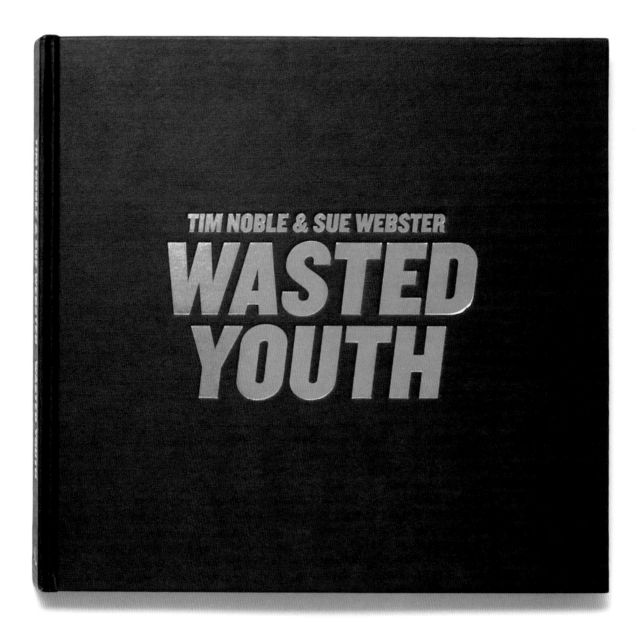

Wasted Youth *book, 2005 (Authors: Tim Noble and Sue Webster; Client: Rizzoli)*

INSTANT GRATIFICATION

YES

KATY MORAN

MODERN ART #01

PUBLISHED BY MODERN ART
10/2006

Katy Moran *exhibition catalog, 2006 (Author: Katy Moran; Client: Modern Art)*

Koenig Books identity system, 2006 (Client: Koenig Books)

MODERN POETRY, RELATIVE POVERTY, AND
EXPERIMENTAL JETSET

The second chapter of Guy Debord's autobiography *Panegyric* (1989)—devoted to his life on the streets of Paris—contains a paragraph that still resonates deeply with us. Right after he quotes the playwright Aristophanes ("I too grew up in the streets!"), Debord states, "After all, it was modern poetry, for the last hundred years, that has led us here. We were a handful who thought it necessary to carry out its program in reality, and certainly to do nothing else."[1]

There is an analogy to be made with our own situation—as an underground subculture of tiny design groups and independent artists trying to carry out the program of Modern graphic design in reality, in the streets of Amsterdam, London, Stockholm, Paris, and New York City. A handful of people dedicated to a Modernist project that started more than a hundred years ago.

We too grew up in the streets, but streets filled with signs and logos created by designers like Wim Crouwel, Ben Bos, and Benno Wissing. Airport signage, telephone books, school atlases, stamps— the visual landscape of our childhood—were designed in large part by Total Design and similar studios. This particular language, so-called late-Modernism, shaped us profoundly, leaving an irreversible imprint on our way of thinking, working, and living.

Moreover, as children we intuitively grasped the poetic dimension that was hidden in this language, a poetic dimension that, to this day, is denied not only by the critics of late-Modernism, but also by the late-Modernists themselves. Crouwel, for example, would never regard his work as poetry. We, who grew up amidst his work, know better.

And so we find ourselves, years later, as graphic designers, working with the cultural material that was handed down to us, rightfully interpreting it in our own way. Critics may regard Modernism as a failed project, but they cannot stop us from speaking the poetic mother tongue in which we were brought up. Modernism might be dismissed as a dead language, but it lives on as a forbidden dialect, spoken in various networks and undercurrents, surviving in fanzines, weblogs, esoteric publishing projects, short-lived exhibitions, and in the day-to-day practice of a small, marginalized subculture of graphic designers.

Unlike people such as Crouwel and Massimo Vignelli in the late sixties and early seventies, we do not head multinational, million-dollar design firms. Instead, we run small operations, working on small

MODERN POETRY, RELATIVE POVERTY, AND EXPERIMENTAL JETSET

assignments. Late-Modernist designers were able to convince themselves, and their clients, that their solutions were the most functional, the most objective, the most neutral. We cannot do that anymore—not to ourselves and not to our clients. It is impossible to call ourselves functionalists, as nowadays functionality is fully defined by "what the public wants"—an empty concept light-years removed from the dialectical stubbornness of Modernism.

Additionally, today's corporations, and even cultural institutions, have been completely taken over by marketing, branding, and communications departments; the last thing they are interested in is the aesthetic or conceptual integrity of the printed object. To them a poster is first of all a parking space for sponsor logos. No wonder that large corporations and institutes would rather work with huge, marketing-driven advertising agencies than with small, ideology-driven design studios.

So where does that leave us? It leaves us barely surviving, living on almost nothing, moving from one small assignment to the next. Owning nothing but our tools and creativity, we are operating in the margins of popular culture, working for a tiny circle of loyal clients. To sustain ourselves we hustle: borrowing money, living on our credit cards, applying for grants. We beg, steal, and borrow through life, all for one reason: to carry out the poetic program of Modern graphic design.

Debord concludes the second chapter of *Panegyric* with the following: "Somewhere between Rue du Four and Rue de Buci, where our youth was so completely lost, as a few glasses were drunk, one could feel certain that we would never do anything better."[2] These words sum up our own feelings. Despite the periods of misery, the relative poverty, the great uncertainty, we know these are probably the best days of our lives. We are producing lots of work, going places, meeting people, writing, teaching, thinking, living. We wouldn't want to trade it for anything else.

Looking at the list of design studios and individual designers featured in *Function, Restraint, and Subversion in Typography*, we are immediately reminded of the German philosopher Ernst Bloch and his words about hope written in *Das Prinzip Hoffnung* (The principle of hope) (1938–47). Bloch insisted that, although the utopian dream might have been shattered, fragments of utopia can still be found in art and popular culture—in architecture, dance, fashion, music, film, traveling, jokes, fairy tales. Each of these fragments contains a utopian potential, a shimmer of hope. Each piece of the puzzle still represents the puzzle as a whole.

The Modernist project might have exploded a while ago, but the fragments remain. The designers and studios featured in this book, each in their own way, contain a utopian potential, a shimmer of hope—an international underground of graphic designers carrying out the poetic program of Modernism, against all odds. We are proud to be a small part of this.

NOTES

1. *Guy Debord,* Panegyric *(London: Verso Books, 2004), 2:22.*

2. *Ibid., 2:26.*

ACKNOWLEDGMENTS

Writing this book has been one of the most challenging endeavors I've ever taken on. It's one thing to say that you're going to write about a certain kind of design because you have some ideas that you've been mulling over. Its quite another to articulate those ideas in a sustained fashion. To see this book completed, and intelligible, is a huge reward for me. I am completely indebted to my editor, Linda Lee, at Princeton Architectural Press for her ability to take the run-on sentences and sometimes-vague ideas that I call writing and hammer them into actual paragraphs that make sense. It couldn't have been easy, and she has my thanks for her insightful comments and questions and most especially her patience. I also need to thank editorial director Jennifer Thompson for getting the ball rolling and bringing the book to Princeton Architectural Press.

The only thing more difficult than writing this book was compiling it. A host of early supporters helped make sure it didn't die before it even started. The efforts of Andrew Blauvelt, Lisa Middag, and Emmet Byrne at the Walker Art Center; Natasha Day and Tony Brook at Spin; Kirsty Carter, Emma Thomas, Louise Ramsay, and Stephen Osman of A Practice For Everyday Life; Marieke Stolk, Danny van den Dungen, and Erwin Brinkers of Experimental Jetset; Colleen Corcoran; and Manuel Raeder were all instrumental in developing momentum for which I'm grateful. And, of course, this book would not exist without the support and feedback of every designer and studio featured in its pages. Thank you so much for your involvement.

Lastly, I'd like to thank my wife and collaborator, Kimberlee, for the support and feedback. We had a newborn baby to take care of while trying to get this book done, and Kim sacrificed a lot of time, energy, and sleep so that I could work on this project. Thank you.

BIOGRAPHIES

AUTHOR BIOGRAPHY

J. Namdev Hardisty is the founder, with Kimberlee Whaley, of The MVA Studio, a boutique creative agency working in design, photography, publishing, and curation for a variety of clients. He is the author of two previous books on art and design, and his work is featured in *Over & Over: A Catalog of Hand-drawn Patterns* (2008) and *Hand Job: A Catalog of Type* (2007), both published by Princeton Architectural Press.

CONTRIBUTOR BIOGRAPHIES

A Practice for Everyday Life (APFEL), founded by Kirsty Carter and Emma Thomas in 2003, is a graphic design studio based in London. The focus of their work is with cultural institutions, often for galleries, museums, and book publishers. They have worked on various projects with the Tate Museum; the Tate Modern; the Institute of Contemporary Arts, London; the Victoria and Albert Museum; and with David Chipperfield Architects for The Hepworth Wakefield. APFEL also recently designed the visual identity for Art Dubai 2009.

Projects and publications by APFEL are held in collections at The Art Institute of Chicago, the Victoria and Albert Museum Archive, Bibliothèque National des livres rares, the Royal College of Art Library, and the Tate Library.

Jonathan Ellery cofounded the London-based design studio Browns in 1998. Browns, which is now run creatively with partner, Nick Jones, has an international reputation based on its ability to mix the worlds of culture and commerce. Clients range from global brands, such as Invesco, Hiscox, Dries Van Noten, The Climate Group, and Channel 4 Television, to small entrepreneurial businesses.

Anthony Burrill is a designer who works in a broad range of media, including print, advertising, moving image, exhibitions, and products. He was born in Littleborough, Lancashire, United Kingdom, and now lives and works on the Isle of Oxney, Kent. After studying graphic design at Leeds Polytechnic, he completed an MA in graphic design at the Royal College of Art, London.

Daniel Eatock was born in Bolton, United Kingdom, and currently splits his time between London, São Paulo, and Venice. An accomplished graphic designer, Eatock applies his former vocational skills to making art. His practice subverts strategies of communications, rational problem solving, and formal design/undesigned methodologies. He uses invitations, opportunities, and chance circumstances, actively seeking, embracing, and responding to the coincidences and contradictions encountered in everyday life.

Xavier Encinas is a French art director living and working in Paris. His work focuses on typography, editorial design, and print collateral and has been internationally recognized for its Minimalist approach and production details. His clients come from fashion, art, and culture industries.

He is design director of the French fashion magazine *Under The Influence* and the Canadian culture magazine *The Lab*. Encinas is also the founder of the typography blog Swiss Legacy.

Experimental Jetset is an Amsterdam-based graphic design firm founded in 1997 by Marieke Stolk, Erwin Brinkers, and Danny van den Dungen. Focusing on printed matter and installation work, Experimental Jetset has worked on projects for Stedelijk Museum CS, Purple Institute, Centre Pompidou, Colette, Dutch Post Group, Réunion des Musées Nationaux, Le Cent Quatre (104), De Theatercompagnie, CAPC Musée d'Art Contemporain de Bordeaux, Bureau Europa, and the Japanese T-shirt label 2K by Gingham.

The group's designs have been featured in a number of group exhibitions, and in 2007, the Museum of Modern Art acquired a large selection of Experimental Jetset's work for inclusion in its permanent collection. Between 2000 and 2009, Experimental Jetset taught at the Gerrit Rietveld Academy in Amsterdam.

Graphic Thought Facility (GTF) is a London-based graphic design consultancy. Established as a partnership in 1990 and as a limited company in 1997, the practice is jointly owned by three directors: Paul Neale, Andy Stevens, and Huw Morgan.

Significant projects include brand identity, signage, and marketing materials for Frieze Art Fair, the Design Museum, Habitat, Marks & Spencer, and The Gagosian Gallery. Self-initiated projects include product design for the Tate Gallery and the Victoria and Albert Museum and GTF's own Mebox storage system.

GTF projects have been included in group exhibitions throughout the world. Their first retrospective, GTF: 50 Projects, was held at DDD Gallery in Osaka in 2006, followed by GTF—Resourceful Design at The Art Institute of Chicago in 2008, the museum's first exhibition devoted solely to graphic design.

Hey Ho was established in 2007 by Julien Hourcade and Thomas Petitjean in Paris and specializes in print design. Since 2006 the studio has art directed for the French publisher Galaade Éditions.

Formed in 2005 by brothers Jody Hudson-Powell and Luke Powell, Hudson-Powell is a design studio in London working in print, inter-active, and motion graphics. Both Luke and Jody studied graphic design at Central St. Martins College of Art (London); Jody continued on to Bartlett School of Architecture (London) to earn and MS in virtual environments. The studio's design principles focus on the dual development of concept and medium with clients in the arts, education, and business. The studio also works on self-initiated projects, which have been shown in various exhibitions including Brno Echo at the Moravian Gallery (Brno, Czech Republic, 2008), Forms of Inquiry at the Architectural Association (London, 2007), and a solo show Responsive Type at SoSo gallery (Sapporo, Japan, 2005).

Zak Kyes is a Swiss-American graphic designer based in London, whose practice encompasses editing, publishing, and curating. He joined the Architectural Association as art director in September 2006 and has curated the touring exhibition Forms of Inquiry: The Architecture of Critical Graphic Design, and coedited the accompanying publication (with Mark Owens, 2007). Kyes has extensively lectured, juried, and taught workshops throughout Europe. He founded Bedford Press, a private press established at the Architectural Association in 2008. He established his own studio, Z.A.K., in 2005 and was recently joined by Grégory Ambos.

MGMT. is an award-winning collaborative graphic design studio based in Brooklyn and Minneapolis. The firm's clients include the International Center of Photography, the American Museum of Natural History, the Guggenheim Museum, the American Folk Art Museum, the Cooper-Hewitt National Design Museum, the National Building Museum, the New York Times, Yale University School of Architecture, and the Anchorage Museum of History and Art in Alaska.

Other projects include the book design of Our Choice: A Plan to Solve the Climate Crisis (2009) and An Inconvenient Truth (2006), both by Al Gore, and exhibition graphics for the permanent collection at the Museum of the Chinese in America (in collaboration with Maya Lin).

BIOGRAPHIES

The principals of MGMT. are Ariel Apte Carter, Alicia Cheng, and Sarah Gephart.

Mike Mills, a graduate of Cooper Union, currently works as a filmmaker, graphic designer, and artist. As a filmmaker, Mills directed the feature film *Thumbsucker* (2005), as well as a number of music videos, commercials, short films, and documentaries, including *The Architecture of Reassurance* (1999); *Deformer* (2000); *Eating, Sleeping, Waiting and Playing* (2003)—a tour documentary of the French band Air; *Not How Or When Or Why But Yes* (2004), as well as a documentary on the music theory of jazz composer Ornette Coleman and several short films for Marc Jacobs.

Rune Mortensen was born in Flekkefjord, Norway, in 1975. After studying art direction and design in Oslo and working for several years at DDB Oslo, he became a freelance designer, focusing on the music and publishing industries. Since 2001 his office has been located inside the jazz club Blå, and he has worked closely with young musicians, authors, and artists. His most recent project is the redesign of the Norwegian literary magazine *Vinduet*.

Mark Blamire, also known as Blam, was born in Carlisle, United Kingdom, in 1969. He graduated from Newcastle College (Newcastle upon Tyne, England) in 1991. In 1997 he formed the successful partnership Groupe, and in 2000 he established his own design studio, Neue. He became one of the cofounders and creative director of Simple Records in 2003. Two years later Blam left commission-based graphic design to concentrate all of his passion and energy into Blanka, an online gallery and permanent visual archive.

Blam lives and works in Chobham, Surrey, with his wife, Sharon, and sons, Jack and Harry. His passions are his family, graphic design, posters, print, and Carlisle United.

Project Projects is a design studio that focuses on print, exhibition, and interactive work in art and architecture. Founded in 2004 by Prem Krishnamurthy and Adam Michaels, the studio's clients include Berkeley Art Museum, Canadian Centre for Architecture, Center for Urban Pedagogy, Field Operations, Guggenheim Museum, Museum of Modern Art, Phaidon, Princeton Architectural Press, Steven Holl Architects, and Whitney Museum of American Art. The studio has received numerous distinctions and was a finalist in the 2009 Cooper-Hewitt National Design Awards. In addition to client-based work, the studio initiates and produces independent curatorial and publishing projects.

Manuel Raeder lives and works in Berlin. His main focus lies in working in close collaborations with artists, plants, scientists, parrots, fashion, designers, printers, interns, librarians, curators, rappers, photocopiers, bookbinders, nonprofessionals (of all kinds), and theorists. His work explores a wide range of formats and examines the boundaries between exhibitions, ephemera, books, type design, editing, publishing, and furniture design. Raeder has held design and publishing workshops at the Ecole nationale supérieure des arts décoratifs, Paris; Université de Toulouse II—Le Mirail; Centro diseño, Mexico City; and the Hochschule für bildende Künste, Hamburg.

Research and Development is a graphic design firm based in Stockholm, Sweden. The members of the studio collaborate with artists, curators, critics, collectors, directors, museums, and cultural institutions to design books, catalogs, posters, exhibition graphics, identity programs, and other printed matter. Research and Development also occasionally arranges film screenings, and produces and participates in exhibitions.

Before venturing out on his own in 2006, Matthew Rezac served as a graphic design fellow at the Walker Art Center. He studied graphic design and photography at the Minneapolis College of Art and Design, where he also worked as part of a small team charged with rebranding the school. His studio and pre-studio work have been featured in *HOW*, *Idea*, *Print*, and *STEP* magazines.

Born and raised in "the cultural void" of South Dakota, his teenage years were spent creating—forming a number of rock bands, booking small punk shows, producing zines, photographing bands, and crudely designing flyers. This DIY methodology continues to shape and inform his design practice.

SEA is a multidisciplinary creative design consultancy founded in 1997 by Bryan Edmondson and John Simpson. SEA has produced a wide range of acclaimed work for clients such as Jamie Oliver, Matthew Williamson, EMI Records, Adidas, GF Smith, Burberry, Boots, and the United Kingdom's largest outdoor clothing brand, Regatta.

Founded in 1992 by Tony Brook and Patricia Finegan, Spin is a company of ten people based in London. The studio is involved in all aspects of the realization of projects from design to production and execution for print, television, and the Internet. Spin has received national and international recognition, winning awards from D&AD and New York Art Directors Club. Clients include Channel 4, D&AD, Deutsche Bank DE, Discovery Networks, Five, Haunch of Venison, ICA (London), More 4, Nike, Photographers' Gallery, Richard Rogers, Sotheby's, and Whitechapel gallery.

Studio Temp, based in Bergamo, Italy, is a graphic design firm established in 2007 by Fausto Giliberti, Guido Gregorio Daminelli, and Marco Fasolini. Studio Temp specializes in traditional print design and also works in web design, motion graphics, and interactive installations.

Since its inception as a modern art center in the 1940s, the Walker Art Center in Minneapolis has maintained an in-house design studio to create all printed materials (more than two hundred projects each year) related to the Walker's communications and publications needs. The studio is the recipient of more than one hundred design awards and has been published and exhibited in the United States, Asia, and Europe. Since 1998 the studio has been led by design director Andrew Blauvelt.

John Wiese is an artist, designer, and composer living and working in Los Angeles. His most recent album, *Circle Snare*, has been released on CD by No Fun Productions and as an LP by PPM. Along with recorded works and collaborations, he has produced typographic scores for large ensembles and multichannel sound installations. His first catalog, *Battery Instruments* (2010), has been published by HSP in New Zealand.

YES is a London-based commercial-art studio founded in 2004 by Simon Earith. The studio works in publishing, music, art, fashion, and broadcasting, creating books, record sleeves, brand identities, printed matter, websites, and motion graphics. Selected clients include A Foundation, Channel 4, EMI Records, Hayward Gallery, Koenig Books, Penguin Books, Phaidon, and Warp Records. The studio also produces an ongoing series of self-published artworks.

Published by
Princeton Architectural Press
37 East Seventh Street
New York, New York 10003

For a free catalog of books, call 1.800.722.6657.
Visit our website at www.papress.com.

Editor: Linda Lee
Designer: J. Namdev Hardisty/The MVA Studio
Design Assistant: Ashley Kapaun

Special thanks to: Bree Anne Apperley, Sara Bader,
Nicola Bednarek Bower, Janet Behning, Becca Casbon,
Carina Cha, Tom Cho, Penny (Yuen Pik) Chu, Russell
Fernandez, Pete Fitzpatrick, Jan Haux, Laurie Manfra,
John Myers, Katharine Myers, Dan Simon, Andrew
Stepanian, Jennifer Thompson, Paul Wagner, Joseph
Weston, and Deb Wood of Princeton Architectural Press

—Kevin C. Lippert, publisher

Library of Congress Cataloging-in-Publication Data
Hardisty, J. Namdev.
  Function, restraint, and subversion in typography /
J. Namdev Hardisty. — 1st ed.
    p. cm.
  ISBN 978-1-56898-966-2 (alk. paper)
1. Graphic design (Typography) I. Title.
  Z246.H365 2010
  686.2'2—dc22
                                        2010018247